NEVERTHELESS

NEVERTHELESS

THE RESILIENCE OF THE MODERN WOMAN

Dana,
Thank you for your
support! Enjoy!
Jillian
Giberson

JILLIAN GIBERSON

NDP

NEW DEGREE PRESS

COPYRIGHT © 2020 JILLIAN GIBERSON

All rights reserved.

NEVERTHELESS

The Resilience of the Modern Woman

ISBN   978-1-63676-570-9 *Paperback*

          978-1-63676-168-8 *Kindle Ebook*

          978-1-63676-169-5 *Ebook*

For every one of my readers. May these women
inspire you as they've inspired me.

CONTENTS

Who run the world? Girls.

- BEYONCÉ

INTRODUCTION

———

**CONTENT WARNING: THIS BOOK CONTAINS
DESCRIPTIONS OF SEXUAL VIOLENCE, SELF-HARM,
MISOGYNY, AND RACISM.**

"Let us be elegant or die!"

-*LOUISA MAY ALCOTT, LITTLE WOMEN.*

I can't tell you exactly what compelled me to take up a professor's offer to join a program that helps students get published, but I can point to exactly when I decided to write the story I am about to tell: I had just finished watching Greta Gerwig's *Little Women* on New Year's Day. In a sense, I grew up with the March sisters. I read Louisa May Alcott's novel obsessively and fell in love with Katherine Hepburn's performance of Jo in the 1933 film adaptation. When I was eight, I toured Alcott's home where she wrote the novel and made it an annual tradition to watch the 1994 adaptation with Winona Ryder's award-winning performance—which has never ceased to inspire me. So when I found myself stuck trying to write a book that I felt I had no place writing, it seemed almost like fate that Alcott's chronicle of four sisters' confrontation with ambition, social norms, and womanhood would reinvigorate my drive to pen a book of my own.

In a time when discussion surrounding gender relations and feminism has become a trending conversation across social media platforms and at family dinner tables, it would seem that a book such as this is simply unnecessary. I had the privilege to grow up surrounded by trailblazing women who taught me the importance of independence and equality. My mom brought me to political rallies while I was still in a stroller. I was raised with women like Hannah Szenes and Rosa Parks as examples of strong female figures who stood up for what they believed in.

Women's voices are being increasingly heard and gender equality is becoming more widely accepted. We've had a woman candidate of a major political party run for president. There are more women with bachelor's degrees than men between twenty-five and twenty-nine years old.[1] So why continue to beat a dead horse? For any woman who has felt the reverberating effects of a patriarchal society, the answer seems obvious. My own realisation of this came to a head when I was preparing for confirmation at my synagogue. My Rabbi had edited all of our speeches that we were to give at the end of the ceremony that Shabbat. To be honest, I can't really recall what I wrote about. But what I do remember is getting my edits back from my Rabbi and

---

1   Alana Semauls, "Poor Girls are Leaving Their Brothers Behind," *The Atlantic*, November 27, 2017.

seeing "he" circled with a comment next to it, that read, "really?" I was taken aback. I was writing as I had seen countless others write before me—using "he" as a generic pronoun. I've never forgotten that moment and, with everything I've written since, that "really?" has remained inscribed in the back of my head.

In her book *Living a Feminist Life*, Sara Ahmed writes of a similar experience and explains, "patriarchal reasoning goes all the way down, to the letter, to the bone. I had to find ways not to reproduce its grammar in what I said, in what I wrote."[2] Part of the project of this book is to help others challenge this omnipresent patriarchal reasoning in their day to day experiences.

Gendered discrimination is alive and well. But what is it? It is important to highlight the difference between gender and sex. Sex is biological, referring to the physiological character-istics or male or female anatomy.[3] Comparatively, gender is a system of culturally defined understandings of men, women, and other identities.[4] Consequently, my experience as a cis-gender woman, meaning my gender identity is the same as my sex at birth, shapes my worldview of gendered issues. I cannot speak on, or write for that matter, the experiences of transgender and other gender-identifying individuals in a way that would do their stories full justice. For those

2   Sara Ahmed, *Living a Feminist Life* (Durham North Carolina: Duke University Press, 2017), 4.

3   Lori Heise, et al. "Gender Inequality and Restrictive Gender Norms: Framing the Challenges to Health," *The Lancet*, May 30, 2019.

4   Lori Heise, et al. "Gender Inequality and Restrictive Gender Norms: Framing the Challenges to Health," *The Lancet*, May 30, 2019.

interested in reading further on gender identity and restrictive gender norms, I cannot recommend Kate Bornstein's book *A Queer and Pleasant Danger* enough.

Sown as seeds from the time children can walk and talk, gender-based social distinctions grow into pertinent questions of self-doubt, in even the strongest of women. At just five, an older boy told me to take off my dress. I was already taught that sometimes bad men will try to touch you or harass you. I knew to say no. I learned the importance of standing up for myself, like when a boy in my second grade class told me he was smarter than me because his dad was a lawyer and I was just a girl.

It took me a while to realize that it was exactly the perpetuation of this self-doubt preventing me from continuing to write this book. I would spend hours writing a sentence, deleting, and then writing it again. More times than not, I would delete that one too. I questioned my validity as a writer, a researcher, and a future author. I was uncomfortable explaining my writing to even my closest friends; I felt like a fraud, worried that they would think it was strange, arrogant even, that I thought I could author a book. So, when I saw *Little Women* that New Year's Day, it felt as if Meg, Jo, Beth, and Amy had been speaking directly to me. It is exactly the lived experiences of ordinary women who struggle with their identity, ambitions, and endeavors that are the important stories to tell, and why shouldn't I be the one to write them?

What follows is a chronicle of my own journey writing this book in my final year of university. It is equally the story of the women in my life whose stories need to be told. It's for the girl who doesn't know if she should go to college, for the survivor who is working to take back her power, for the student whose college years went by in the blink of an eye and is now on the cusp of the rest of her life.

CHAPTER 1

MAKING AND TAKING UP SPACE

———

I raise up my voice—not so that I can shout, but so that those without a voice can be heard. [...] We cannot all succeed when half of us are held back.

- MALALA YOUSAFZAI

What the hell am I doing here, I remember thinking from my seat as I watched the other women file in, stopping at the front table to grab a name tag. For anyone who has participated in sorority recruitment, you'll understand what I mean.

I would be remiss if I didn't mention just how impactful joining a sorority was on me. It was not something I ever saw myself enjoying, but in the months leading up to my first year at McGill University, the only thing my friends seemed interested in talking about was whether we were going to join a sorority. I figured why not give it a try, although in the back of my mind I figured I would drop after orientation.

The whole process felt like a fever dream and before I even decided that this was something I wanted to do, I was being whisked into the final day of rounds and on my way to the Kappa Kappa Gamma house. Aside from focusing on not breaking my ankle in my new heels, I was half-paying attention to a conversation I was having with another tall, blonde, and beautiful girl who had just transferred to McGill from some American state school—*Typical.*

She introduced herself as Jane and then immediately began gushing over how amazing the girls were at Kappa and that she already met who she knew would be her best friend—*Typical.*

The next morning, I—along with a new friend Anne who lived on the floor above me— trekked to the center of campus. Anne was impossibly cool: she was from Miami and had a wardrobe I would kill for. We got our "bids" and after a cringeworthy countdown from ten, everyone ripped open their envelopes and ran to the cheering crowds of their respective sororities. I looked down and felt a wave of relief. Kappa. I looked at Anne and she smiled; she got Kappa too— *Thank God.*

Suddenly a flash of blonde hair and blue glitter nearly tackled me to the ground—Jane. *How did she already have blue glitter?* I smiled, gave her a tight hug back, and was promptly led to get my new shirt. The rest of the day was even more of a blur. Blue frosted cupcakes and taking a nauseating amount of pictures stand out.

What amazed me was how readily everyone welcomed us in, and—to my surprise—I felt a jitter of excitement and honor to be accepted so quickly. There was only one face in the crowd of new members that I was a bit hesitant about. The last time I saw her, she was standing outside of our rez on moving day with no less than four industrial pallets of maple-flavored baked beans—*Questionable*. With more energy than I think I could ever muster, she introduced herself as my new neighbor, Bailey. And now we were sisters—*Great*.

An important side note: this is not to neglect the problematic and elitist nature that Greek life tends to perpetuate. Over my three years in Kappa, we've worked hard to distance our chapter from the complex history of Greek life, its overall lack of diversity, and the gendered dynamics that all too often feed into a dated and heteronormative culture between sororities and fraternities. Regardless, there is something extraordinarily empowering to be in an organization built by and run by women. We have a long ways to go in ensuring that these spaces are inclusive and safe for women from all backgrounds and it is important to highlight such institutional problems, regardless of how welcomed you may have felt in such a space.

Looking back, the judgments I passed on nearly everyone who would become my closest friends were laughably off base. Jane would become my best friend and one of the strongest women I have ever had the privilege to know. Anne, who remains ever-so cool and wears the cutest clothes, has proven to be one of the smartest people I know. Mia, who I initially knew as the quiet girl I recognized from my dorms, has become my confidant and support system. Between the two of us, we have shed more tears over grad school apps and job applications than I could have thought possible. And Bailey, the crazy bean girl, is still in fact a crazy bean girl; it's been nearly three years and she still has some cans leftover, but has also become the most incredible friend.

I could go on. I have been introduced to some of the most incredible women through these connections, about whom a book could be written about each. Quickly, I became close with a number of older members who helped guide me through those tumultuous few months that is freshman fall. One such sister was Violet. She had just founded the first Canadian chapter of It's On Us at McGill, an extraordinary organization that works to create dialogue surrounding sexual violence, intersectionality, and gender relations on campus. It was Violet who taught me the importance of making and taking up space.

* * *

When I committed to writing the stories of real women who have faced extraordinary circumstances, nearly two years after I first came to McGill, I didn't have to look further than my own circles. It occurred to me during this process that even in the most exclusionary environment—especially taking classes where you could go an entire semester without reading any piece written by a woman, much less a person of color or from a non-western narrative—we have managed, in our own ways, to take up space.

I was in the early stages of writing the first draft of my manuscript when I sat down to interview Violet. When I tried to explain what I was writing and why, I must have been projecting a sense of self-doubt. I kept including disclaimers like, "this isn't like an actual book, just something to add to my resume," or "I don't expect anyone to actually read it, I just think it could help me get into law school." She looked at me:

"You are allowed to take up space, but you need to make space for others as well."

It took me a long time to come to terms with this and the intentions behind my writing. I know now that hearing this would be a turning point for me, both in the writing of this book and in my academic career as a whole. Throughout this entire process of writing, deleting, rewriting, and editing this book, it was my self-doubt that stayed the most consistent. I knew these stories and my stories deserved to be told, and the voices of real women deserve to be heard; but the question always lingered in the back of my mind: why should I be the one to tell them?

I told Jane what Violet had said. "I get what she means, but I'm not sure how I could 'make space for others too.'"

"Jillian, you just finished writing a story of a sexual assault for this. You are opening the door for more stories to be told." Sure, but for some reason I still felt a bit of a fraud.

Much of this derives from the complex history of white feminism and the role I see myself in. Intersectionality, especially concerning race and sexuality, has been often left out of the narrative of mainstream feminist movements. As a result, the voices of many women of color have largely been silenced and there remains significant disparities not just along gendered lines, but racial ones as well. I cannot speak on behalf of these women, I can only make space for their own voices to be heard; and in an effort to do so, I've been intentional in including quotes and works from women of color. I go more in depth on the importance of including intersectionality in any feminist project specifically in chapters eight and nine as well.

Yes, "published author" is a fantastic addition to my resume; but more importantly, I am using my voice and taking up space that I have a right to. I am privileged. I was given this opportunity and took it on a whim, admittedly for selfish purposes at first. But this is also an opportunity to tell the stories of the women around me who have made it possible to write this to begin with. I should be the one to tell them, because I can.

My undergraduate experience, from a purely academic perspective, has really been defined by two dichotomous fears: that I do not participate enough in class and that I am not qualified or intelligent enough to speak up when I did. Lacking confidence and feeling inadequate, I have often marveled at—and at times envied—the students who were so willing to voice their input in conferences and lectures. Over the years I have found many of my friends, particularly women, feel the same way. We are driven by a need to prove to ourselves that we can, but are restricted by our fear of appearing aggressive or too ambitious. In short, there is pressure to maintain a level of humility.

This realization came to a head when I found myself complaining about a conference I had to attend for one of my classes. There was a girl who I decided I immediately didn't like on day one. She sat right next to the TA facilitating the discussion and seemingly had an answer for every question. I have a rule when it comes to participating—I try to speak three times throughout the conference to secure my participation mark, and maybe if I feel like I have something important to contribute I'll speak up more. That rarely happens.

So, this student particularly irked me. I couldn't understand who would think so highly of themselves to participate so frequently. As I have come to realize, my first impressions of people tend to be way off base and, as I was with my new sorority sisters, I was wrong.

CHAPTER 2

WOMEN SUPPORTING WOMEN AND OTHER MANTRAS

———

A feminist is anyone who recognizes the equality and full humanity of women and men.

- GLORIA STEINEM

It's hard to admit when you're wrong. My roommates and I were huddled around a single laptop screen watching one of the early Democratic Primary debates when it hit me. After seeing the likes of Kamala Harris and Amy Klobachar get nearly half the speaking time that the debate frontrunner enjoyed, I realized I had never really complained about the men in my conferences who participated frequently.

Sure, when they begin a response to a question about privilege with "to play devil's advocate," I tend to roll my eyes. But looking back, I could never recall losing my patience with a guy for taking up too much time.

I would be lying if I said I was not ashamed to admit this. As Madeleine Albright once said, "There is a special place in hell for women who do not support other women." But no one's perfect. Often, we are pitted against each other in a race to trail-blaze and shatter those glass ceilings. It can feel like a competition—that no matter what we do, there is always another woman who has done more to advance our gender.

What we fail to see a lot of times, whether it is in a conference or in the workplace, is that feminism is not a zero-sum game. One woman's successes, or participation points for that matter, do not come at the expense of another's. And I think that's what Madeleine Albright is hinting toward: that we are allowed to take up space, but we also have to make space. And while the simple mantra "women supporting women" won't relieve us of generations of socially learned biases, it can serve to remind us of the importance of creating space for our fellow women, even with those that we have the most complex relationships with.

Jane—that bubbly blonde transfer from the States—and I were catching up after summer break, following her internship at a marketing firm and my summer term at Cambridge. At our favorite coffee spot just a short walk from campus we scrolled through pictures from our travels and eventually found ourselves nearly shouting about the woes of social media.

I was angrily reminiscing on how, after I shared a picture in a bathrobe, a family member commented on the appropriateness of the post. Having spent much of her summer in marketing, Jane nodded in agreement. Social media has a unique and powerful role in creating dialogue surrounding ideas of modesty.

"I hate that I have to take into account what I wear in a photo for the sake of my career when there are Supreme Court nominees with accusations of sexual assault levied against them who seem to be doing just fine professionally," I wrote in a message later that day to another friend in marketing.

Jane recounted experiencing something similar. Always smiling, Jane's Instagram profile perfectly conveys her confidence and sense of style, with cropped, blonde hair framing her freckled face. Her page, with its remarkable color coordination and witty captions, has a number of pictures on the beach or at a pool. In some, like most personal profiles of twenty-something year olds, she is wearing a bikini. She recalls countless arguments between her and her mom about her photos and why she refused to "cover up."

These complex and often intergenerational differences between how we perceive the importance of modesty, have played out in countless forums between any number of women. The very public nature of a platform such as Instagram especially, fuels debates over what constitutes an "appropriate" picture or one that a future employer might see and decide you're too much of a slut to be hired.

Beyond Instagram posts, Jane and I both agreed that we've witnessed the stark intergenerational divide between us and our parents or grandparents in terms of feminism. The introduction of first and second wave feminism into our conversation, required another round of lattes.

Jane reflected on her grandmother's successes in politics at a time when women rarely had a seat at the table. She was extremely influential within Canada's conservative party and was often the only woman in photos with her political peers. As she grew up, however, Jane recognized that her political views didn't often line up with her grandmother's.

"It's complicated in terms of pride. She was in that arena when a lot of women weren't; but at the end of the day, her views remain very much conservative—especially as they relate to gender." Jane paused. "For example, in regards to sexual assault, she doesn't really recognize it as a perpetrator issue, but rather a victim's issue."

As a survivor herself of sexual assault, this is an especially sensitive subject. "It's one thing to be asked what you were wearing by the police, but it's different when your grandma blames survivors for what happened based on their clothes."

I have found a lot of women especially struggle with reconciling the views of first and second-wave feminism with contemporary gender issues. On campus, we often talk openly and frankly about more complicated issues when it comes to feminisms: sex work, intersectionality, and creating a sex -positive environment free of kink or slut-shaming. Yelling "drunk sex can definitely be consensual and it's FUN" is probably not the kind of activism my mother or grandmother envision I would undertake in university. A huge part of this book for me, however, is perpetuating this kind of dialogue and recognizing the importance of addressing even the most uncomfortable or controversial subjects.

* * *

I had crowd-sourced potential stories of women that people knew on social media and I got an influx of responses. Emily, a friend and sorority sister, reached out and said her mom was a trailblazer in initially controversial campaigns: including movements that addressed abortion, sex-workers, and the destigmatizing of STDs.

Emily's mother, Audrey, was at the heart of the fight for reproductive rights in Canada. She worked at the only abortion clinic in the greater Toronto area, which was set to be raided at any time. Audrey, along with her co-workers and fellow activists, used the inevitability of a raid to directly challenge the illegality of abortion in Canadian federal law. When the raids began, Audrey started a phone tree: a common form of activist communication prior to cell phones. Everyone had a list of people to call when they got the call, who would then make their own calls.

Before continuing, Emily laughed and noted that it sounds just like those pyramid schemes we see on Instagram today.

Following her respective calls, Audrey ran over to the clinic that was just four blocks from where she worked during the day, prepared to be what Emily called a "raid protector." The phone tree had mobilized hundreds of others, who ran over and blocked the police from entering the clinic. They not only covered the entire property surrounding the clinic, but also blocked the sidewalks and subway entrance. Emily recalls her mom explaining how she was kicked and shoved by police officers.

The raid and subsequent response was a major catalyst in bringing the case of abortion to the Supreme Court. The resulting case, *R v. Morgentaler,* would hold that the provision regarding abortion in the Canadian Criminal Code was unconstitutional.

I said something about being impressed and began to thank Emily for her time. "No there's more," she laughed.

Audrey was not just on the forefront of the fight for reproductive rights in Canada, she was, and still is, a staunch advocate for LGBTQ+ rights and sex workers. She was especially involved in mitigating the AIDs crisis in Ottawa in the early '90s, soliciting funding and donations to keep clinics running.

At one clinic where she worked, Audrey helped a man write his will after his family disowned him following his diagnosis. She coached another woman on how to tell her daughter she was positive. She ran funerals for those with AIDs who had no one else to organize them, and rallied communities to come together and attend so there were people in attendance. Audrey was on the frontlines advocating for others far before it became normalized to do so.

When Emily concluded, she said something that has stuck with me: she was upset that she knows she'll never be able to do anything like her mom has. To that I say: there are always new fights to be had, new wars to be won. I think Audrey's story is an incredible example of advocating for what you believe even before it becomes a mainstream issue. Hindsight is 20/20 after all.

And there is so much to be advocated for today. A huge issue that I've worked to dedicate my time to is addressing the prevalence of sexual violence in our political and social environments. My own interest really evolved with the growing presence of the Me Too Movement in the fall of 2017 in tandem with my first semester as McGill. I was especially inspired by the work of survivors in raising awareness, both on campus and in the larger public sphere. I thought it was absurd that survivors had to come out as victims to raise awareness and confront the parasitic nature of gendered and sexual based violence in our communities. I didn't think it was fair.

It is important to note that the Me Too Movement was originally founded by Tarana Burke in 2006. Though popularized ten years later by high-profile celebrity posts, Burke—a woman of color—saw her initiative take off with little credit attributed to her. Again, this follows a similar trend of mainstream feminist activism excluding the narratives of women of color and the integral role that intersectionality plays in understanding contemporary gender dynamics.

One of the incredible dimensions of activism in 2020, in contrast to Audrey's experience in the early '90s, is the reach of social media. With the click of button, you can have a world of knowledge at your fingertips. And a simple share is all it takes to publicly profess your own social concerns.

Initially, sharing posts and the like felt like enough. As the Me Too Movement progressed, however, I began to see the flaws in our ability to simply click "share" or post about an issue and consider your part done. I wanted to be able to do more, to take concrete action.

I changed my major from Middle Eastern Studies and dropped my Arabic course, which admittedly was kicking my ass as is, and changed to a double major in political science and international development studies. I wanted to study the role of gender in international relations and pursue a career advocating for women's rights within a legal and global context.

Studying toward a career I was passionate about turned out to be a game changer for me. I loved my classes and was determined to do well in them, not just for the grades, but because I actually wanted to put what I learned to use.

In my spare time I began reading the memoirs and biographies of some of my own role models. These included Madeleine Albright's *Fascism: A Warning* and Malala Yousafzai's *I am Malala: The Girl Who Stood Up for Education and Was Shot by the Taliban*. Especially inspiring was Michelle Obama's *Becoming* and its emphasis on the value of education inspired me to look into graduate school opportunities.

One of the most consistent themes I saw throughout my courses was the exclusion of women in the formal economies of developing countries. My interest in how women are incorporated into political and economic theory was further encouraged by a gender and international relations course—one of my all-time favorite undergrad courses—that highlighted just how excluded gender was from mainstream theoretical narratives. But I'm getting ahead of myself.

CHAPTER 3

THE POWERFUL MOMENTS ARE THE POWERLESS ONES

CONTENT WARNING: THIS CHAPTER INCLUDES REFERENCES TO SEXUAL VIOLENCE.

Justice is about making sure that being polite is not the same thing as being quiet. In fact, often times, the most righteous thing you can do is shake the table.

- ALEXANDRIA OCASIO-CORTEZ

One of the most important and impactful movements I have been a part of is the fight against sexual violence on university campuses. Pervasive and taboo, the discussion surrounding sexual violence in a university context is messy and frustrating, with nearly every one of the women I know experiencing it to some degree.

I remember a group of friends and I went out to brunch the October of my senior year. It was cool and classes had just begun to pick up as September gave way to chilly days and soft, light jackets. We were at our favorite restaurant with an unmistakable bronze ceiling, lush hanging plants, and industrial light fixtures. It was during a particularly tense time regarding sexual violence on campus; Channel Miller had just come out as Jane Doe in the Stanford rape case that had made international headlines over the past couple of years.

There was something cathartic about resigning our Sunday to day drinking and eggs benedict amid the controversies of campus life and just before the impending onslaught of midterm exams and papers.

We raised our champagne flutes, "To midterms!"

In addition to taking on research for this book, I was particularly stressed with trying to find an advisor for my undergraduate thesis. Inspired by a course I took over the summer, I wanted to pursue a topic exploring the role of peacebuilding and international law in intra-state conflicts. I had been directed and redirected countless times between professors, each with a different academic niche that would fit better with my proposed topic. I was at my wits end.

"Guess who I was referred to on Friday," I took a sip from my glass. I had been thrown into student activism early my first year when a movement calling for the university to take more substantial action regarding sexual harassment cases levied against professors and TAs was taking campus by storm. The names of three accused professors became infamously connected with the protests and I learned early on to avoid, at all costs, taking one of their classes. My reference, of course, was to one of those professors.

"She told me he was probably the only professor in the department whose research fit my interests," I sighed. Jane raised an eyebrow. "I don't know what else to do other than to completely change the direction of my thesis."

Anne pipped in, "Honestly, I refuse to take a class with him. If the administration isn't going to hold him accountable, I will."

"Yeah, I dropped a class of his in first year," my roommate Mia agreed.

Anne refilled my glass. "Ok, but how is it ok that I have been put in the position of deciding between pursuing the thesis topic I wanted or completely change directions because I refuse to work with a professor accused of sexual harassment," I protested. Quite literally I, a twenty-year old undergrad, was being asked to hold a professor more accountable than the administration itself.

Before anyone could respond, our food arrived. Half an omelette later, my friend Alex spoke up. "You know something similar just happened to Kate. She started that new internship at the hospital this week and one of the doctors keeps flirting with her."

Mia nodded in agreement, "She said a nurse came up to her later and said something about him liking her.

Apparently, he flirts with all the new interns, but not to worry because he's married and wouldn't actually do anything. He's harmless."

The whole table grimaced. He's harmless. Right.

It seemed everyone had a story. Jane said she had a TA who at the end of last year asked for her number and to see her over the summer. Then she had him again next semester. "It was so uncomfortable, he only knew my name and would always call on me. I was honestly just scared that people thought I was sleeping with him to get an A."

"I honestly had no idea this was an issue at first," Alex mused. "It wasn't until Violet told me about one of the protests that I found out about it. I know so many girls who have never heard anything about it."

* * *

It was in fact Kappa that introduced me to the world of campus activism. At first, I was skeptical—especially with getting involved in the messy politics of sexual violence and gender relations on campus. When Violet first explained to me what It's On Us was trying to do on campus, I was nervous. What could the repercussions be? What would people think?

It seemed safer to stick with something less controversial. I limited my involvement on campus for the first semester. While I focused on my adjustment to university life and course load, however, I began to realize the extent to which sexual violence was prevalent on campus.

A number of articles came out in the years leading up to my first year at McGill, all of which talked outwardly about the inadequate responses the administration had taken regarding issues of sexual harassment. My friend sent me an especially poignant article written in a student-run newspaper in 2015 during my first year at McGill that fundamentally changed my perspective on campus life as a whole.

It was written by an anonymous student who had an affair with a professor on campus for over a year and a half. She wrote out the story beautifully, of how their relationship started off seemingly natural and well-intended. As a fairly naïve first year, I was shocked.

The name of the professor and of other perpetrators the author referenced throughout her piece remained anonymous. That said, the names of a few professors had become infamous around campus and luckily I didn't have any classes with them; however, I couldn't help but wonder how many others have done the same thing that we don't know about.

I especially hated going to office hours with male professors my first year. I knew myself and didn't think I would be able to do anything but comply if put in a similar situation. I was terrified of jeopardizing my academic career and as a wide-eyed freshman, I valued what my professors' and TAs' thoughts of me above anything else.

Looking back, my dichotomous fear of and admiration for my professors seems silly. I've learned that standing up for myself can't harm my academic career unless I let it. Being an outspoken advocate for myself and the students around me has been more valuable to my education than any A on a transcript could be.

My second semester I began working with It's On Us McGill (again, a new organization that Violet began on campus and the first Canadian chapter). And so it began.

Advocating for and working with sexual assault survivors is enlightening, draining, and inspiring all at the same time. At times you want to give up. Other times you want to scream and take to social media in a flurry of rants. Following events such as the Kavanaugh hearings can make it feel like you play such a small, insignificant part in a fight that seems all but a lost cause.

Over the years, our executive board has gone through thick and thin. We have held workshops where we have been challenged and berated, being asked to justify our statistics and definition of rape. One participant asked how to tell his girlfriend to "get over it" after she disclosed she was sexually assaulted the summer before. Another asked what the actual legal definitions of sexual violence were: how much could one get away with?

At times it was shocking, knowing the level of ignorance and apparent indifference that existed within our own community. Despite first year programming that introduced discussions surrounding sexual violence on campus, many of these conversations failed to continue outside of mandated consent training.

* * *

In a number of my conversations with various groups on campus, I have also come to realize that there is an overall sense that some sexual violence is worse than others. For example, I had a conversation with a friend from the States, Danielle, about finding out that people you know have been accused of some form of sexual violence. She told me about an old friend who had been accused of assaulting and harassing multiple students at their high school. Then she casually dropped that the last time she saw him, he tried to do the same to her.

I asked what she meant. Danielle had explained she was friends with him throughout high school. He was a year younger, and would occasionally ask uncomfortably intimate questions but she didn't think much of it. When she went off to university, they spoke every so often, and at one point he accidentally sent her a nude. She brushed it off and took his word.

"During spring break he really wanted to hang out and because he was a good friend in high school, I figured we might as well," Danielle recounted. She picked him up from their school and they grabbed food. "On the drive home he was like 'let's just pull over in a parking and I'll rock your world…give you the most amazing sex of your life,'" she grimaced. He was extremely persistent, but she kept saying no and tried to ignore him for the rest of the drive.

When they got back to campus, Danielle told him she was waiting to meet up with another old friend. "While I was calling her, he started touching me in places he shouldn't have and I swatted him away and then pretty quickly got out of the car." She said goodbye and after an uncomfortably long hug, they parted and she left to find her friend. "I played it cool but knew I was gonna block him on everything and never see him again."

Only a month later, she was talking with another former classmate when they told her he had been accused of sexual assault and harassment by a number of students, mainly freshman girls. He had been student body president of their private school and, given how assertive he was, she could see how these younger girls would have been coerced by him. "I guess I just had a slightly different power dynamic so I wasn't as vulnerable," she concluded.

"Ok, but that's still disgusting," I said. "He may not have raped you, but he violated you and your body after you repeatedly said no."

She shrugged, "I still feel lucky...comparatively."

Power dynamics are funny things. We talk about them often during our workshops with groups on campus, especially on how they go beyond professor-student relationships. In any organizational structure there are hierarchies in place that can easily translate into other relationships.

The classic example we use are older-student leaders and freshmen during orientation week in early September. As new students, freshmen are especially vulnerable to coercion by older students, and the administration works extremely hard to put measures in place to prevent the development of such relationships until the week is over.

To me, it seemed obvious that these conversations were crucial to have. I know too many people, women and men alike, who had experienced some degree of sexual violence, both on and off campus.

Mia was followed by a man in a red van masturbating while she was out walking one morning. There was a series of attempted trafficking incidents on and around campus. Alex had been stopped twice by the perpetrators. Another man on campus began following women from the library late at night touching himself.

One time, after being cat-called by two cars in a row just a block from our apartment, Anna came home fuming. Our household was in the middle of passing around Chanel Miller's memoir *Know My Name* so we were especially sensitive to incidents of sexual violence, both in the media and in our own lives. "I don't even get mad anymore when it happens, it happens so often," Mia and I nodded in agreement. "It's insane to me that this is something people think is normal and ok to do." We nodded again.

"Imagine if there was a Google doc or something with the name of every man, ever, who has cat-called someone," Anna mused. "I mean Google would crash immediately, there would be so many entries." We laughed.

I added that there was something almost cathartic about living through a pandemic when everyone is a bit uncomfortable going outside: "I mean, welcome to our world." It reminded me of something my friend Claire had said when I was interviewing her for another chapter of this book. I asked what experience defines being a woman to her. She thought for a moment and then looked up, "For me, the powerful moments are the powerless ones."

CHAPTER 4

...ALIENS?

Women, if the soul of the nation is to be saved, I believe you must become its soul.

- CORETTA SCOTT KING

Accepting your voice and taking up space is not a linear process. After I had resolved to write the stories of the women in my life and established my own goals for this book, the writing process was still wrought with doubt. There were times when I spent an hour writing one paragraph just to delete it in the end. And then there were the times when others made me question my own place and voice.

I had spent the day rushing from class to class, writing bits and pieces of my first story for the first chapter of this book, and studying for an upcoming midterm. By the evening I was exhausted. I had plans to grab drinks for the first time with a guy I had just met and, to be frank, the idea of drinking a couple of gin and tonics to end what felt like my very own day from hell was growing more and more appealing.

The date began like any other with those awkward getting-to-know you chats. We really could not have been any different. He was an older Australian circus performer and I was an American student studying political science and international development.

My experience as an American studying abroad has often been an interesting point of conversation and, while my mom always warned me to never talk politics on a first date, I often find myself fielding questions regarding American politics—especially the 2016 election.

Never afraid to talk about my own political leanings, especially as they relate to my degree, I was honest. No, I did not choose to study in Canada because of Trump's victory. Yes, it is hard to watch. Especially from afar.

I was blunt. For a lot of Americans, Clinton's loss was devastating, and I like to think the result of the 2016 election is not reflective of what I consider to be integral American values.

Then the conversation shifted. "Well don't you think that Trump was, like, just a little bit better than Clinton, between her emails and everything. I mean did you really want her to be your first female president?"

I was taken aback. How do I explain that her gender didn't make a difference? That it came down to her experience, his lack of experience, and their comparative policies?

He pressed further. "Ok but there are biological differences between men and women. Like psychologically. And men are just biologically predisposed to holding leadership positions, you know with their aggression."

I took a deep breath and a sip, or two, from my drink then dove in. There was a lot that I could cover: beginning with the fact that yes, sex is biologically determined by a balance of hormones, but that gender itself is a socially learned identity, and not exactly the ideal characteristic to draw assumptions regarding one's ability to lead. And then of course there is the question of whether aggression or other typically "masculine" attributes are important traits for political leaders to have. At risk of digressing on a theoretical tangent outlining all the details of feminist international thought, I simply said one's gender doesn't play a role in whether they'd make a good leader.

He persisted. "Ok but what if aliens came down tomorrow? Who would you rather have in office, a man or a woman?" If I am being perfectly honest, I think I laughed, then asked if he was being serious. I could not believe that in 2020 this was a question I was actually being asked. And there it was: my own powerful powerless moment.

* * *

Ironically, as I write this in the time of the Covid-19 pandemic, it appears many of the countries that are successfully limiting the spread of the virus are led by women. According to a study published in June 2020, COVID-responses and containment were systemically better in countries run by women.[5] Par-

---

5   Supriya Garikipati and Uma Kambhampati, "Leading the Fight Against the Pandemic: Does Gender 'Really' Matter?" *SSRN,* June 3, 2020.

tially explained by coordinated policies, proactive responses, and clear communication, countries with female heads of state, including Germany, Norway, and New Zealand, have experienced fewer cases and less loss of life.[6]

I also can't help but wonder: *what if.* The 2016 Presidential election was devastating not just to me, but for Americans across the country. As a woman, it was disheartening, to say the least. It was one of those flashbulb moments.

During that election cycle I had committed about a year and a half interning for a congressional campaign in New Jersey. On election day, I spent a few hours at our offices making a last-ditch effort to get voters to the polls. It was one of the tightest congressional races in the country and the DNC had sent in volunteers from all over the East Coast. It was nerve-racking. We were running against a long-time incumbent in an unpredictable district in the far north of New Jersey. There were as many Trump signs as there were for Hillary.

In retrospect, the outcome of the presidential election shouldn't have come as a surprise. In my high school, kids were touting Trump shirts and MAGA hats, but they seemed more the exception than the rule. One kid flew a Trump 2016 flag from the back of his truck. *Ridiculous*, I thought. But I was wrong.

Amongst those in the campaign, we all but knew Hillary would win. All of our anxieties revolved around the

---

6   Ibid.

Congressional elections; there were a number of New Jersey districts we thought could be flipped from red to blue.

While I was finishing up my outreach calls, one of the DNC volunteers from DC was packing up to go and said, "We are about to elect the first female president, remember this day." I smiled.

I responded with something along the lines of, "I'm so anxious about this district I can't be excited about Hillary yet." Which was true. I finished making my calls and said farewell to the staff I had worked under for the better half of two years. They were getting ready to go to an election night event with local party officials. Admittedly, I was a bit jealous. I would have given anything to be in a room with people who had dedicated countless hours to the 2016 races when Hillary won, and hopefully, when we flipped our own district.

All things considered, I'm rather grateful I was at home without all of the pomp and circumstance. Somehow, it lessened the blow.

When I got home, I situated myself in front of the TV with CNN—or maybe it was MSNBC—settling in for an evening of anxious nail biting. I had the *New York Times* pulled up on my laptop and I was switching between Twitter and sending a flurry of messages on my phone.

I was following the district results so closely I almost missed the tide of the Presidential election turn. By 8:30, we knew we had won the district. I turned my attention to national polling. A friend, whose mom works closely with the DNC as a consultant, sent a message in our group chat from summer camp. "If Hillary loses Pennsylvania, we lose the election."

My stomach must have done some sort of backflip. *Wait what? It is not supposed to be this close.*

Florida. Michigan. Ohio. *Jesus Christ.*

By midnight I decided to go to bed. Maybe it would all be better in the morning. It had to be. I woke up at 6:00 a.m. to an onslaught of news notifications. "Donald Trump will be the 45th President of the United States." I don't know how long I sat there for, staring at my phone. I know I didn't have time to eat breakfast.

At some point I had to have gotten up and ready for school. On the way, we passed the handful of lawn signs that we had grown accustomed to seeing on our street. Suddenly each one stood out. *Trump, Trump, Hillary, Trump, Clinton, Kaine. Make America Great Again.*

I passed a number of MAGA hats and Trump t-shirts in the hallways. At lunch, the same pick-up truck I had laughed at just the day before sped by me, the Trump flag and an American flag picking up the wind behind it.

The rest of the day was just a blur of articles explaining the upset from every news network I could find. For the most part, I couldn't understand the complex polling data, graphs, and figures. Maybe there would be a recount? Surely this was some kind of mistake.

Looking back, my experience in that bar with the Australian man makes an excellent bad-date-story to tell over a bottle of wine and popcorn with friends. But it also represents a major turning point for me in my academic career and in the process of writing this book. The privilege of learning and living on a fairly progressive campus insulated me from the gendered realities of the real world, one where women's agency and abilities are constantly challenged and questioned. It was a huge wake up call for me and reminded me why this book needed to be written.

Okay universe, note taken. So, I got back to work on my research and took to social media reaching out to as many women as I could from an array of diverse backgrounds and experiences. What does it mean for you to be a woman? What experience defines womanhood for you?

I received an influx of incredible responses. I spent the next week immersed in stories of resilience, harassment, self-doubt, self-confidence, and everything in between. I have never felt more empowered. But, it was equally emotionally draining, and I found myself struggling to decide what to include and how.

* * *

One of my favorite, and perhaps most unexpected connections, came from my friend Julie in Louisiana. An aunt of hers was a trailblazer in local politics and had been involved since the '70s. I asked if she would be willing to do a phone interview and later that day I got a call from a Louisiana number.

On the other side of the line was Kathy, with one of thickest southern accents I have ever heard. I was excited to not only speak with an older woman who had begun her work during the second wave of feminism, but also a southerner who undoubtedly lives in a very different political reality than I do.

After a brief introduction, I explained how I conducted most of my interviews. Beginning with my intentionally broad questions, I welcomed Kathy to start with what comes to her mind first when asked what feminism meant to her. "Professionally," she explained, "it would be working as the chief of staff for the first woman mayor of my small, southern city."

"We had the opportunity to be in leadership capacity in a world which was predominately male. Department heads as well as other leaders within the city; obviously the other council members were all men," she began. Obviously.

I asked how she became involved in local politics. Was it something she studied in school? Kathy chuckled and told me she was actually a mathematics major, "not a typical female major," and began working with early computing programs.

"I was always charting a path in college in not-typical female programs like our friends who did art history," to which she quickly added, "which is a great thing to do but more typically 'female' than mathematics." I smiled. Nearly half a century later, you can still see a significant gender divide between disciplines: there are times when a friend of mine in engineering is the only woman in her lab.

Kathy explained that she found her way into local politics after her community experienced a wave of labor violence. "It was a very desperate time in the community, and much trauma," she described. "We decided that it was time for a change and elected public leadership, and as a result of that, my idealistic husband ran for district attorney."

By the '90s, they were effectively ingrained in local politics, and Kathy was asked to run for the first female mayoral campaign in their city's history. I asked if she had been at all influenced by the second wave feminist movement that was just beginning when she was a college student.

Kathy casually explained that she organized the first women's conference for her region. "We were not at the bra-burning edge of doing the more radical feminism," she laughed. "But yeah, we were in the community working to bring women together for the purpose of adding to cultural discussion."

I asked why she wouldn't consider that radical. At a time when she was expected to stay at home, she was bringing together women from all backgrounds, races, and religions for a conference that would continue to be held to this day. How many conversations did she help spark? How many friendships did she help forge?

I think sometimes, especially as women, we have a hard time accepting that what we do can be impactful. I see this all the time in my conversations with survivors of sexual assault. There is nothing more powerful to me than using your voice and advocating for others, even after such trauma.

All of the women I spoke with have shown incredible strength, and I think if I were asked again who I would rather have in office during an alien invasion, I would choose any of the women whose stories I've had the privilege to write.

CHAPTER 5

TRAUMA, SURVIVORSHIP, AND EMPOWERMENT

CONTENT WARNING: THIS CHAPTER SPEAKS IN-DEPTH ABOUT SEXUAL VIOLENCE AND SELF-HARM.

The barricades that held us down will not work anymore. And when silence and shame are gone, there will be nothing to stop us. We will not stand by as our mouths are covered, bodies entered. We will speak, we will speak, we will speak.

- CHANEL MILLER

I knew that no book addressing gender and empowerment would be complete without the integral narrative of survivorship. These conversations with survivors of sexual assault were especially difficult. In my writing, I walked a very thin line between including the necessary information without sensationalizing or dramatizing these very real experiences.

Consequently, the following chapter includes stories of rape and abuse. They were among the most difficult pieces I have had to write and are equally as difficult to read, but they need to be told.

Working with survivors of sexual violence on campus has been one of the most profound and enriching experiences of my time at McGill. As one of the founders of It's On Us always says, being a survivor of sexual assault is like being a part of the shittiest club in the world, but it's filled with the most resilient, beautiful, and strong individuals.

Trauma is derived from being powerless, but for so many of the survivors I know, in its wake an enormous amount of strength can be found. Claire, one of the co-presidents of It's On Us in my senior year, is a shining example of that. My favorite part about my job with It's On Us, other than talking about sex with a room full of fraternity brothers, is making space for survivors to take back their power and share their stories. For Claire, it is about living her truth, rather than the shame. No matter how messy that truth may be.

Everyone told Claire that she was going to love university. And for her first year she remained enamored with this ideal of collegiate life. After that first year, she moved into an apartment with her best friends in what students call "The McGill Ghetto." The name is deceiving. A four block neighborhood that leads directly into McGill's downtown campus, the Ghetto is lined primarily with old Victorian brownstones that have been converted into smaller apartments. In terms of location, they couldn't have found a better apartment. The entrance of campus was just across the street and almost all their friends lived within two or three blocks of each other. Even at 2:00 a.m., the streets feel safe and familiar: as if it was in its own bubble, safe from the tumult of downtown Montreal.

About to meet up with a group of her friends, Claire threw on a nightgown and grabbed a bag of pretzels. It felt silly, but she called her best friend and asked that she stay on the phone while she walked, even though she was just two blocks away. Not five meters from her front door, Claire heard someone running behind her. It was an odd time to go for a run, but she didn't think much of it. And then she felt someone pick her up from behind.

Assuming it was one of her friends who lived nearby, Claire began to laugh. And then they turned a corner into an alleyway. Confused, she heard her friend ask what was going on through the phone. But what you don't learn in sixth grade biology class is that when threatened, there is a third instinct after fight or flight: it's freeze. The man, dressed in a dark hoody and gloves, dragged her down the alley by her feet.

After what felt like hours, but was really only minutes, she started to scream and her friend, still on the line, came running. It was only then that the man stopped. In Claire's words, "He said 'thank you' after doing his thing and then ran away."

He said thank you.

It was only after he left that her flight response kicked in and she ran back to her building where she locked herself in her room. "I just became a ghost for a bit."

The panic set in after her friend found her and called her mom. Four male police officers were sent to her apartment. A note: research shows that who someone discloses their assault to and how their disclosure is received can change the trajectory of their entire healing process.[7] This would come to be a critical part in her survivorship experience.

The officers began with standard questions: what happened exactly, did you get a clear look at his face, and so on. Then they asked if she was wearing underwear. Claire was honest, yes she was wearing a nightgown with no underwear.

They raised an eyebrow. Suddenly, it was as if the officers thought she deserved it.

Then they began flirting with both her and her friend.

After fielding compliments on their eyes and height, they made it to the hospital where Claire would spend over five hours waiting on doctors and test results. In the months following, she experienced what so many survivors do: the indifference and inefficiency of a bureaucratic academic institution and the administrative nightmare that is a police investigation. Refusing to take any official action because the assault didn't technically occur on campus, McGill suggested she take a twenty-five dollar self-defence course they offer once a semester. She was advised not to talk to professors because they did not yet have a training program on receiving disclosures.

---

7   B. R. Marriott, C. C. Lewis , R.L. Gobin, "Disclosing Traumatic Experiences: Correlates, Context, and Consequences," in *Psychological Trauma: Theory, Research, Practice, and Policy* 8(2), 2016.

Thereafter, Claire would wake up from nightmares about the assault and there were times when she would ask herself why he didn't kill her. But as time went on, her nightmares became less frequent, her bruises faded, and after three months, the police closed the investigation having never caught the perpetrator. Trauma manifests itself in sneaky ways, however, and she turned to alcohol to manage her anxiety.

Ten months later, substance abuse became a way to prevent severe flashbacks and anxiety from undiagnosed PTSD. One morning, she took all the antidepressants she had; in all, it amounted to about one-hundred-and-fifty pills. When her mom found her, she was rushed to the hospital where she was placed in an induced coma for three days. She remained in the hospital for another two weeks.

When Claire first told me her story in full, she stopped at this point and gave me a sarcastic grin. "It's really sad that it took me almost dying to really hit rock bottom and realize that changes needed to be made."

At this point it had been nearly a year since the assault. She was sober for six months and began to channel all the anger and anxiety that had crippled her for the past year into something positive. The following semester she went back to school. When she was ready to finally confront what had happened, there weren't many resources offered that she thought could help. That's when she found It's On Us.

It was in her interview for a position on the 2018 executive board that she truly felt supported by her peers and an on-campus organization. As she explained to me the impact of her experience getting that position and working on the board, she paused again, this time to chuckle. "It has changed my life. I don't want to say dramatic because I don't want to minimize my feelings, but I want to say it really has changed my life. It has helped me heal and make me feel understood."

When she concluded her story, I asked Claire if there was anything she wasn't comfortable with me writing. She didn't skip a beat, "I'm pretty open with everyone about this. I think that's part of me, fighting back against the shame and the guilt that I feel with both the overdose and the assault.

"It would be easier to hide it, but my own healing process was largely reading about other people's stories, and how they've come through the other side. I want to live my truth, I really do."

Claire's is a story of incomprehensible strength and courage. Like all of ours, it is riddled with ups and downs. It's messy, but as Claire said halfway through our interview, "Hey, so is life."

* * *

Like Claire, working with survivors has transformed my life. It has challenged my understanding of feminism, of privilege, and of the culture surrounding gender and sexual relations. Claire and I often lead workshops together with various organizations on campus: fraternities, sororities, and varsity teams, etc. When I first began presenting on consent and bystander intervention, I was shocked at how basic some of the content was. To be honest, I was nervous most of the students I spoke with would find it insultingly simple.

When presenting to largely female-identifying groups, I always ask, "By a show of hands, who has asked their guy friends to pretend to be your boyfriend at a bar?" Always, at least half of the room's hands go up. When I ask the opposite to male-identifying groups, the ratio is usually about the same. Then I follow up with why.

"Usually the other guy won't take no for an answer," is the typical response.

I press further, "But what changes when you bring another man into it? Why is a simple 'no' not enough?"

This is where we tend to get stuck. A simple, though admittedly disturbing, way of understanding this is by thinking in terms of property. A single woman is "free" for the taking, regardless of her own preferences (the concept of female agency doesn't often connect with those who don't hear "no.") If she is in a relationship with a man, however, she "belongs" to him. It is an antiquated concept but still very much embedded in our perceptions of gender roles. It has become almost instinctual for me to immediately say that I have a boyfriend when in such a situation.

This has been played out time and time again. Last year, the entrance to Mia's boyfriend's apartment was down a dark alleyway off a busy street in downtown Montreal. It was already dark when she got there one evening and as she waited, a man approached her. We've all had that moment: increased heart rate, avoiding eye contact, praying he just walks by. He asks her for her name, says she's really beautiful, and that he just wants to get to know her. She grimaces. "I'm waiting for someone, sorry." She says.

He doesn't stop, in fact he comes a little closer. "What's the matter, I'm complimenting you."

She looks away. Where is Brian? Luckily, he turned the corner just a couple of seconds later, taking the stranger aback. Oh. She's taken.

When they got inside, Brian chuckled and said something about the guy probably being drunk or high. He didn't get it. But when Mia recounted the experience to Anne and me a few nights later, we knew exactly what she had felt. We all agreed that we would never lease an apartment down an alley to begin with, especially not downtown. To Brian, however, that was hardly a concern; maybe it wasn't as aesthetically pleasing as a brownstone, but there was never a concern for his safety.

I have found that nearly all the women I talk to have had similar experiences. Our responses have become nearly second nature. And, while I am hesitant to declare this a "silver lining" because there really can't be one in the perpetuation of sexual harassment as a norm or just fact of life, I do think such experiences can strengthen and empower us to advocate for change.

Elaborating on her definition of womanhood, Claire reminisced, "The powerful moments are the moments when those norms are being fought against." She recalled the Women's March in Montreal, "I was there, screaming, 'my body my choice,' just for the mere fact that we are women. We will be seen, heard, and believed."

The powerful moments are the powerless moments.

Regarding her assault, Claire explained, "Trauma happens when you're powerless. I wish I could say that I got to do this because I'm a woman and I got this platform to change the lives of other women." For Claire, it was her circumstance, being sexually assaulted, that gave her voice volume. It is ok to feel the most emboldened by the moments meant to knock you down the hardest. Sometimes, empowerment can be derived from trauma.

CHAPTER 6

LAST HIRED, FIRST FIRED

There's something so special about a woman who dominates in a man's world. It takes a certain grace, strength, intelligence, fearlessness, and the nerve to never take no for an answer.

- RIHANNA

This writing process has introduced me to a number of incredible women. This led to a fascinating conversation with the founder of a professional consulting firm that works specifically with women at various stages in their careers, Randi Braun. We spoke primarily about the power of social media in supporting female agency and upward mobility, while also wielding the risk of reputational damage.

Randi explained the permeating effects of socialized gender norms. "I work with a lot of high performing, high potential women and their biggest struggle isn't the quality of their work or the impact they are making, it is their ability to tell the story about that work in a way that projects confidence and ownership." She notes that social media opens a lot of opportunities for women to position themselves as leaders, but in a way that seems less threatening to others around them. There is something about the function of social media that allows for many women to confront their imposter syndrome and professional anxiety.

I immediately understood what she was referring to. Updating my LinkedIn profile is far easier for me than going in person and asserting all of the leadership positions I've had. Randi agreed. She has worked with countless women who struggle presenting in person to their boss a list of their accomplishments from the past say, six months. It is so much easier to take to Twitter or LinkedIn to update their portfolios.

When I spoke with Randi, I was in the midst of applying for graduate schools. Naturally, an integral part of that process is reaching out to professors and peers for letters of recommendation. When I went in-person, one professor asked me why I was applying for graduate school and why I thought I would be a good fit. I froze.

I had the grades. I had the motivation and the desire to learn. But I couldn't translate that into why I thought I deserved a spot over someone else. Especially not at a school like LSE or Cambridge. I'm sure I managed to stutter out a decent enough explanation—after all he agreed to write the letter.

Of course, social media has had its fair share of negative reverberating effects through the professional and public world. There is the concept of what Randi called, "reputational risk." Our ability to reach a mass audience with the click of a button makes things like revenge porn far easier to derail an entire career.

This is not to say that imposter syndrome alone is what holds women back academically and professionally. I spoke with my friend Rachel whose parents are both academics in Montreal. Their story plays out almost as a natural experiment on the ways in which gender discrimination can permeate into our careers, despite our achievements and intellect.

Rachel's parents met while completing their undergraduate degrees. They went on to move to Canada together to complete both their masters' and PhDs in sociology.

They went to all the same universities. They did all of the same programs. Their CVs looked almost identical, except that Rachel's mom actually had a higher overall GPA. By all accounts, my quantitative research methods professor would deem that a near-perfect natural experiment.

When it came time for both of her parents to get jobs, they both began as research assistants and slowly started getting positions as lecturers. That's when Rachel's father's career really took off.

He rose in the ranks of his respective university and enjoyed a number of promotions. By forty, he was a tenured professor.

For those unfamiliar, that is remarkably early in academia. But what about her mom?

Despite their nearly identical resumes, Rachel's mom struggled to get hired, even for entry-level positions within university administrations. She has still never achieved full professorship, remaining a lecturer and student advisor throughout her career. For Rachel, a university student in engineering (a field with even less women than one such as sociology), this is extraordinarily disheartening.

"My mom is this incredibly intelligent, bright woman. She has so much to say and it's frustrating for her to see my dad get tenured so early." Her mom actually left the first university she worked at because, despite going for as many promotions as possible, she was never able to move up.

Today, her mother works as a part-time professor and academic advisor. She loves her job and has done incredible work, but has still never achieved full-professorship. To this Rachel added, "My mom works her ass off. Students love her, and then there's my dad who actually hates teaching. He's one of those resentful professors, but he still has a salary four times higher than my mom."

I decided to research this further. According to research done at the Université de Montréal in 2018, of the women in the Canadian academic community, forty-eight percent are assistant professors and forty-one percent are associate professors. Only twenty-six percent are tenured.[8]

---

8   Anabel Cossette Civitella, "Women Academics are Still Out Numbered at the Higher Ranks," *University Affairs,* June 13, 2018.

The numbers for women in the natural sciences and applied maths are even starker. According to a 2012 study done by American researchers at the National Academy of Sciences, the mean salary offered to women applying to a science lab managerial position was just over $26,000. Male students applying to that same position, with comparable applications, were offered over $30,000 as a base salary. As Kathy had said, such subjects were not, and clearly still aren't, considered "female majors."

* * *

Today, the social sciences and humanities have drastically more female representation, but that has not always been the case. My mom has always boasted that we come from a family of writers. Her cousin Rieva Lesonsky is perhaps the shining example of such. Born in Brooklyn in the early ⬛50s, Rieva was the first of four children and raised equally by her parents with a love for sports, especially baseball and hockey. "I remember thinking, 'why can't I play little league;' I was better than most of the kids on my brother's team," she recalled in our first interview.

That was the first time, but far from the last, that she felt there was a difference between the way that she and her sisters, Robin and Jayne, and her younger brother, Ronnie, were treated.

Rieva had been on the student council her entire middle and high school career. By sixteen she knew she wanted to go to university. In response, her school guidance counselor asserted that she could go on to study to be a teacher. "I said, but I don't want to be a teacher," Rieva recalled.

"He got immediately exasperated and said, 'Well you can be a nurse.' I laughed, I hadn't even wanted to dissect a frog in my biology class," she continued. "He said, 'You can be a secretary, though you're too smart to be a secretary and should really be a teacher.' This was in 1967."

Rieva thought about what to say to him. "I remember seeing women's names in the bylines of the *New York Times*, so out of nowhere I said I wanted to be a journalist. Out of desperation really." She recalled that he seemed startled. And that was when she realised that there were really only three options; that there was an assumption that if you were a woman, you could either be a teacher, nurse, or secretary. That's it.

"My generation had to continually fight that. It was tough to find a job, it wasn't about credentials, it was how fast you could type."

RIEVA LESONSKY.

Women weren't hired, they were relegated to certain roles.

To pursue this newfound dream of journalism she went to the University of Missouri. She recalled the professor of her magazine journalism class explaining that "there are the seven sisters," a group of women's magazines—such as *Good Housekeeping*—all of which were edited by men. "That shocked me," she said.

But Rieva didn't want to pursue a career in women's magazines anyway. What she really loved was sports. "I knew everything about sports," she recalled. "The thing I loved the most back then was baseball. So my inclination would have been to be a sports reporter, probably. But I was one generation too soon." The first woman sports reporter for the *New York Times* would end up being only two years younger than Rieva.

She had also worked as a newscaster for her school radio station, but wasn't allowed to lead the sports section because she was a woman. She recalled the one time that she did broadcast that section: "The head of sports found me and he said, 'Just do it. What are they going to do?' So I did it one day just because he said, 'You got it.'"

I asked if there was any backlash to her doing the sports news. Rieva laughed and responded, "No, there was no reaction to that and I think that was just part of a step in the evolutionary process. Like, why not, you know? Who cares?" She added that the station was really only broadcast in the dorms, so their audience was exclusively students. As student broadcasters for the university radio, they were left largely unsupervised; so Rieva and Jim, the head sports newscaster, made up a story to explain why she took over that day—just in case someone, presumably on faculty, questioned it.

It's funny—no one was worried about the student reaction. And looking back, it was quite obvious that times were changing, but in the moment, the tenure of the older, more conservative generation seemed in many ways, unbreachable.

* * *

Today, the obstacles women face, both at school and in the job market, while perhaps less glaring and seemingly archaic, are still incredibly pertinent. The gender pay gap is one such example. Despite countless protests and efforts to ensure equal pay, overall, women are not making the same as their male counterparts. I asked Bailey, who has had to work multiple jobs to support herself through high school and pay for university, if she has experienced this. "I mean yeah, of course," she responded matter-of-fact with an unsettling air of nonchalance.

"The worst was probably when I was working at McDonalds and had to replace a manager quickly," she explained. "I basically had to learn how to do the job in a week and didn't get the raise in pay that came with it until like three months after." She continued to explain that the guy she replaced was still being paid the same managerial salary as her.

"When I was just a crew member too, my raises were never as high as the guys, even though I consistently got excellent reviews." Bailey grimaced, "I guess I didn't really realize how bad that was until now..." I shook my head. How is it that we've become so conditioned as to not fight back?

For Bailey, at seventeen, she was just happy to have a job. I asked her if she would have done anything different looking back. She thought for a minute and said, "Overall, at McDonalds, while it was the worst job I've ever had, I also learned the most there than I had in any other job."

First jobs tend to have that effect I find. My first time working in a restaurant, as a hostess, was extraordinarily eye opening. I was nineteen and working on the main street of Provincetown in Cape Cod, Massachusetts, at the peak of the summer season. The town was always packed; but especially on the weekends when my manager often told me to stand outside and try to get tourists to come in.

During the week when it was less crowded, I became familiar with the locals. One older man lived on the street next to the restaurant and would always go for walks and drives past our entrance. My first day standing outside he pulled up next to curb in his silver minivan and rolled down his window to say hi. He whistled and yelled, "Who are YOU?"

I smiled politely and waved. "I'm the new hostess," I responded, unsure.

He said, "Honey you do not need to work there, marry me and I'll give you everything you need! Wow are you beautiful." I was embarrassed, mainly because a couple that had just walked by turned around and gave an inquisitive look. I laughed it off and said thank you, hoping that he would drive away.

He waved again and said he'll see me around—*Great.*

I went in and asked the bartender—who had become my de facto mentor for all things Provincetown-related—who he was. He laughed and said "Oh, that's just Bill, he's harmless. He proposes to me every other week." I gave him the benefit of the doubt and went on with my day.

Bill walked by every day, usually twice. Sometimes he would just wave and wish me a good afternoon. I was always relieved. Other times he would stop uncomfortably close to me, grab my hand and say, "Gosh you're beautiful." I would laugh it off and say thank you so I could get back to work as quickly as possible. I got in trouble if I spent too long speaking with a local. I think he proposed to me about once a week.

Other men would comment that they only came in because I was so pretty. One guy said that if he was twenty years younger, he "would be all over me." I tried my hardest to brush them off and go about my day, worried that if I said anything my manager—a cantankerous older woman who called every hour to make sure I was still standing outside handing out menus—would get angry. It was a temporary position as I was heading to Cambridge for the rest of the summer at the end of June, so I held my tongue.

I didn't realize it at the time, but I think this experience really drove me to focus on gender roles in my writing of this book and in a number of my research projects over the past year. Bill especially served as a reminder that no matter how strongly I speak out against harassment and sexist standards, there are times when I too let it get the best of me and am too afraid to speak up. And that's okay.

CHAPTER 7

COURSE CODES AND DRESS CODES

———

The success of every woman should be the inspiration to another. We should raise each other up. Make sure you're very courageous: be strong, be extremely kind, and above all be humble.

— SERENA WILLIAMS

A few days before I had a call with my managing editor for this book, I woke up early to study for a midterm. Furiously going through my flash cards and bouncing back between lecture and readings notes, an email notification popped up on my phone. *Your LSE application to the MSc in International Political Economy.*

My heart skipped a beat. *I have to sit for a midterm in less than an hour and I'm about to get rejected from grad school—Nice.* I apprehensively opened the email and it took a second for my eyes to focus on the words.

Congratulations! I gasp and reread. I yelled for Mia from the couch, "Um I just got into LSE...I think." She shrieked, I think I probably did too, and Anne emerged from her room.

I showed them the email to confirm that I hadn't hallucinated it and, flashcards forgotten on a cushion, I called my mom. Somehow, I made it to my midterm on time.

I hadn't let myself imagine getting into any of the graduate programs I applied to, bracing myself for those seemingly inevitable rejection letters. I had already gotten rejected from a program at Oxford that was marketed toward experienced policymakers, and reading the email felt almost as though some prophecy had been fulfilled. *Of course you were rejected. You are a twenty-year-old undergrad with no experience... applying to Oxford.*

So, I had low expectations for my application to the London School of Economics. I had already begun bookmarking potential jobs in London so I could at least still move there after graduation like I had planned, even if I got rejected from every academic program. After I was accepted, I still couldn't quite convince myself it was true. It wasn't until nearly a week later, when I got a follow up email from my department offering their congratulations, that I began to believe it wasn't some sort of mistake.

Ironically, as I was convincing myself I was in no way qualified to get into a grad program, I was writing the first few chapters of this book on self-doubt among women, especially in academia. I felt a bit like a fraud every time I went to write the story of another empowering woman who beat the odds and earned her degree in mathematics or chemistry. I was sure I wasn't smart enough or accomplished enough to get accepted, all while I was encouraging other women to pursue their passions and take on the obstacles of academia.

Jane was especially beating herself up over the prospect of applying for postgraduate programs. While my own admission was still pending from LSE, I was trying to convince Jane that she could totally get into law school. I remember looking at her exasperated one day while she weighed the pros and cons of even trying to take the LSAT.

"I know my GPA isn't good enough for McGill or Toronto, but if I really grind for the exam, maybe I could get into a second-tier school or something." I continued trying to convince her to at least take the LSAT and see what she gets. I had the utmost confidence in her; I still do. But like me, she was unable to even imagine herself getting in, why should she even try if she had no chance?

Like so many women I know, we are so averse to believing in our own accomplishments and value that we are the ones often standing in the way of ourselves. As I've already confessed in early chapters, perhaps to a fault, convincing myself that I could write this book has been perhaps the most difficult part of the process.

While I was in the writing process, Mia would often send me the occasional article she came across in her psychology courses on gender relations. We had been discussing how relatively few female authors and theorists we had to read outside of gender studies courses, when she remembered a study she had read a few days before.

Behavioral Ecology, a scientific journal, had conducted a series of double-blind reviews of academic papers so that the reviewers did not know the name of the authors. The results showed a significant increase in publications by female authors after the double-blind reviews began.

When I sent the piece to Jane, she sent back the syllabus of a class that listed only one woman author for a semester's worth of required readings. How do we recognize that our own academic pursuits are legitimate when we have so few examples of women who came before us?

I am realizing now that much of my doubt surrounding my own place in university stems from this. Since my first year, I have doubted my ability to write articulate papers or say something constructive in conferences. In my first year, I debated writing a research paper on how fashion can be an effective form of communication for female politicians. I spoke with my TA and said I was concerned it wasn't an important enough topic for a university-level political science course.

I don't remember exactly what she said, but I decided to go for it. And I got an A.

Looking back, it's funny that I was concerned I couldn't write a university-level paper on women and clothing considering how vehemently I have advocated against dress codes and questions surrounding what victims of sexual assault were wearing—of course it is important. In the docu-series *Hillary*, there is a clip of Hillary Clinton laughing that, in total, she spent twenty-five days of her 2016 presidential campaign getting hair and makeup done.[9] Just because something isn't talked about much in an academic setting, doesn't mean it's not important.

* * *

When I spoke with Lauren Goldberg, an attorney and mom to one of my close friends, she brought up the role clothing has played in her own career. "My parents used to say that it doesn't matter if you're not comfortable, just look the part. And so I got really good at that."

Lauren recalled how her mom asked if she was really wearing sweatpants while she was on her way to the hospital due to a respiratory infection: "I couldn't breathe, but you know it was the idea that on the outside, everything should look perfect." This is an extreme example, but it really resonated with me. How many times have we dressed up to portray this perfect woman, when on the inside we are actually struggling.

"That theory of living isn't a good one," Lauren added. "You're putting yourself out to the world as one thing, but you're feeling like another as if the only thing that matters is outside. You need to be able to have that inside comfort with yourself."

In addition to being the managing attorney of a firm, Lauren also frequently works with local political leaders, especially

---

9   *Hillary*, "Be Our Champion, Go Away," Episode 4, directed by Nanette Burstein.

female politicians. When I brought up *Hillary*, she nodded knowingly.

"You know what's crazy about it is that I think she was in a damned if you do, and damned if you don't, kind of situation." We talked about how the professional clothes of the eighties for women included massive shoulder pads in suits just like menswear. "It was like if you can shut off that female thing, and look powerful, you'll be someone else's equal," she surmised.

And Hillary Clinton was a perfect example of that. She did everything right to look and act like the professional woman: she withheld her emotions, she was always put together, she demonstrated her intelligence. According to Lauren, "But people, they couldn't relate to her because she didn't act emotional at all. And in the big picture, had she, people would have said she's hysterical and not practical."

I asked if she still saw that reservation in the women she worked today. Lauren nodded. "I can see how hard they are working to keep their feelings out of it," she said. It is one of the big differences she sees in working with women and men. Men are quick to respond intensely, with anger or excitement. Women tend to remain more restrained. "I tell them just say what you think, it's fine," Lauren laughed, but noted that there is always something holding them back: a fear of being seen as too emotional.

I can feel that same restraint in my own writing. With every story I tell or every point I try to make, I'm worried it sounds peevish or annoying. The inclusion of such emotions, however, is exactly what makes this something readers can connect to and know that there is a real person behind these words. We are our own worst critics and I'm no exception to that.

I have had moments of self-doubt throughout my university career, who hasn't? But I have found myself increasingly questioning my right to opportunities and programs even after I've been accepted in. Like LSE, when I got into Cambridge for a summer program, I told myself they probably accepted everyone, it's just a summer program after all.

When I got there and met my peers from top-tier US schools, ones I would have never even considered applying to in high school, I felt like a fraud. I sent a series of anxiety-ridden texts to my friends at McGill about feeling so out of place. I said something about John Maynard Keynes rolling over in his grave knowing I was studying in the King's College library.

My first few days there were surreal. I was astonished at the sheer grandeur of the university and its many colleges. I spent an absurd amount of time exploring the library at King's which, I'm sure comes as no surprise, boasted impressive architecture and an even more impressive collection of books. It was overwhelming and it wasn't until I was sitting in a classroom, notebook open and pen at the ready, that I could I really picture myself as a student there.

I'm not sure when I realized I could fully hold my own at Cambridge. By the end of my summer there, however, something had changed for me. I had done well in all of my courses and my peers who I was most afraid of became some of my best friends. When I looked around the King's dining hall at our last formal dinner, I saw that the paintings of some of Britain's most important academics lining the walls were all men. But as I looked around at my friends, it was a table made up nearly entirely of women.

So yes, my university experience hasn't been entirely absent of empowering women. Far from it. I have had a number of incredible professors that I have looked up to throughout my courses who epitomize not just strong, inspiring women, but brilliant academics as well.

CHAPTER 8

AT THE INTERSECTION
OF FEMINISM

———

I am not free while any woman is unfree, even when her
shackles are very different from my own.

- AUDRE LORDE

I should have expected that going to school in Canada would
provide a uniquely international experience. Even more so,
the culture shock of coming from a public high school in New
Jersey to a massive university in Montreal, was surprisingly
intense—and it began almost immediately.

On our first day of orientation, the student body president
began his speech with a land acknowledgement. As I would
learn, before any event and most classes, McGill acknowl-
edges that it is built on the traditional land of the Kanien'ke-
hà:ka, one of the many indigenous tribes in Canada. Looking
back, it's almost comical how confused I was. But as an
American student coming from a high school whose mascot

was quite literally an "Indian," I had never experienced such accountability on behalf of an institution. Of course, through my courses and time living in Montreal, I've come to learn that land acknowledgements are simply the bare minimum in the reconciliation of a colonial past, but it's a start.

In addition to some degree of institutional accountability, McGill also introduced me to countless extraordinary students from not just Canada, but across the globe. Eyitayo Kunle-Oladosu, the editor-in-chief of the political science journal I worked for in my last year, was one of those uniquely international students—having been born in Nigeria, but raised in Ontario after immigrating at just six years old. I was eager to interview her not just because of her position as EIC for our journal, but also for her involvement in Model UN.

Just around the time I interviewed her, Eyitayo was working on submitting an appeal to the Commission on the Status of Women as the head of the Model UN delegation to the commission. Regarding the inquiry on missing and murdered Indigenous women in Canada, the appeal highlights that Canada has failed to publish a national action plan over the past year. In explaining her passion for involvement in these projects, she stated, "Youth are critically underrepresented in international space when it comes to decision making, not to mention racialized youth, indigenous youth, youth from low income backgrounds, and youth from the LGBTQ+ community."

The importance of incorporating young voices into international policy cannot be taken for granted. It is often students and young people who are the first to support new and growing discussions surrounding issues of gender and intersectionality. Eyitayo's work is critical in sustaining these conversations and holding institutional actors, such as the Canadian government, accountable in upholding their promises to address gendered and intersectional issues.

While the number of female students grows, and in some areas surpasses that of their male peers, academic discourse and courses are still largely directed by the work of men. Take my discipline of international political economy. The field, an offshoot of international relations, was developed in the '90s, primarily by renowned British scholar Susan Strange. But if you were to take an IPE class today, or even an entire MSc program like myself, you would hardly know that.

I spent the last few weeks of my summer balancing preparations for my first semester at LSE with the revisions period of this book. I noticed immediately that the course preliminary readings were all written by men, and that the majority of the offered courses failed to include the work of any female scholar in their indicative readings list. How Strange...pun intended.

I decided to look more into Susan Strange's work; her name was only familiar through one course I had taken at McGill. A simple search of her name really tells you all you need to know about academia's view of her. One of the first articles that popped up on my Google search, was "Susan Strange: A Great Thinker or 'Journalist.'" Hm.

There is a debate in the social sciences as to what counts as legitimate "methods" of studying intangible ideas such as governance and human behavior. Critics would argue that Strange's lack of clear research methodology or proper citational efforts (i.e. using statistics to understand a phenomenon or referencing other such works) demotes her work to journalism rather than scholarly theory.

But that entire debate does something more than discredit a single academic's work: it can, and has, excluded countless others, mainly women and people of color, from contributing otherwise ground-breaking work within a social science setting. Sara Ahmed, a leading feminist writer and independent scholar, explains this as such: "I have known feminist examiners of feminist dissertations ask for more white men to be added to reference lists…simply put, if academic fields remain organised around white men, then to be respectful of history, to cite right, to cite well, can in practice translate into a requirement to cite more white men."[10]

"Citations are academic bricks; and bricks become walls."

SARA AHMED.[11]

Why talk about this? Students of political science, especially women and people of color, are not unfamiliar with this concept. However, many of these conversations exist only within the discipline and are not accessible to those who aren't actively studying the subject. Diversity of thought is lacking in nearly all disciplines, but far too often "progressive" institutions tout

---

10 Sara Ahmed, "White Men," Feministkilljoys, accessed September 20, 2020.

11 Ibid.

their initiatives to increase accessibility and inclusion all the while assigning works done primarily by white, prominent men.

In my conversation with Eyitayo, we talked a lot about this phenomenon. She makes a point of picking courses with female historians and to use sources written by women and people of color. She agreed that in our disciplines, history and political science, women and especially women of color are grossly underrepresented.

She said something that I had never quite realized, but related to right away: "I find that when we do read things by women of color, those are articles, those are the pieces, that are cutting edge, right? They're pushing the envelope."

We take the female academics, especially women of color, we are exposed to for granted. They are the ones that are not only breaking barriers in getting their work published at all, but often, they are pioneering new perspectives and even at times, new disciplines. Just like Susan Strange.

And so, to combat this phenomenon of academic exclusion, Ahmed offers the simple solution of citing fewer cis-white men. "We can rebuild our houses with feminist tools; with de-colonial precision we can bring the house of whiteness down," she writes.[12]

Of course it's not fair to negate the work of white male academics all together. But it is important to note that the

---

12   Sara Ahmed, "White Men," Feministkilljoys, accessed September 20, 2020.

obstacles faced by women and academics of color, has forced them to break into the conversation with new perspectives. In the introduction to *On Being Included*, Ahmed states that "whiteness tends to be visible to those who do not inhabit it."[13] This can be attributed to gender as well and it is important in this project of framing obstacles women and people of color encounter to recognise that just because we cannot initially see the issues at hand does not mean they are not there. Take the time to look around the table. Who do you see? How many white faces do you see? How many men are there?

This is especially pertinent in humanities and social science disciplines such as history. Eyitayo explained how such disciplines can be enriched by new perspectives: "People think that history is stuck in one time, but in everything we're learning, our understanding of what happened in that period changes and there are different paradigms of understanding one particular period."

"In my experience, women are the ones who are saying okay we thought this was what happened, but we need to rethink this relationship between these two actors, because there's a dynamic that you're not understanding," she continued. Specifically on work and historical fields dominated by men, Eyitayo notes that "there's a trend to observe everything with a black and white framework."

In a similar field, political science, what is extraordinary is that fifty percent of the population, fifty percent of citizens,

---

13   Sara Ahmed *On Being Included* (Durham: Duke University Press, 2012), 13.

fifty percent of consumers, etc. are essentially excluded from mainstream theory. Traditional paradigms of thought in the social sciences have largely been developed by white male academics and consequently, reflect that experience. One of the few theories that intentionally addresses this concern is Feminist theory.

As Ahmed writes, "In reflecting about gender as a relation, feminist theorists offer critical insight into the mechanisms of power as such, and in particular, how power can be redone at the moment it is imagined as undone."[14]

You may ask yourself, why is she telling me this? *It doesn't matter to me, I'm not a political scientist or historian. I didn't even study this in university.* To that I say this: this elite and exclusionary group of thinkers do not just write obscure articles and teach university courses. They act as policy advisors and lawmakers, and if not, their works are informing and training our future leaders every day. And when you are exposed only to theories reflective of the white male experience, more often than not, that is how you too are going to look through that lens. Policies developed under that white-male gaze cannot solely solve pervasive issues such as systemic racism and the gender pay gap.

Modern problems require modern solutions. Well, modern policy issues require modern solutions driven by those who are disproportionately affected by them and have also been historically excluded from the conversations.

---

14 Ibid.

But publications and policymaking are not the only areas in which women and people of color face significant discrimination. Misogyny and subconscious biases have permeated academia at a micro level as well: they are present in every classroom.

In explaining her effort to pick primarily female professors, Eyitayo highlighted another interesting phenomenon that exists amongst even the most progressive of student bodies. Every university student is well-versed in ratemyprofessor. com, an unbelievably insightful and handy tool when choosing courses. But it is also reflective of the double standard female professors face in the lecture hall. Eyitayo points out, "There's an expectation that women are kind and have to coddle you, and like, you know, she's not your mom right, she's just a professor and you can't expect her to treat you like a baby through the course."

Such double standards exist not just within the reputations of professors, but in even getting a seat at the table to begin with. I had the privilege of growing up in an environment where girls were largely treated as having the same intellect as boys. In my schooling, I never felt the pressure to do well because I was a girl, because I had something to prove. Extremely telling is that both Kathiana and Eyitayo, who are both Black women, spoke on the pressure to not just perform well, but to excel. That mediocrity is not an option.

It goes further than just excelling, however. There is a pressure to filter nearly every word published or social media post posted so as to not unintentionally sabotage your own professional or academic image. Eyitayo reflected on a recent article in which she really began to realise the weight of this. "I recently wrote something about police violence, I literally had like three different white people read it over," she explained. "We've made some progress, but we can never really have the freedom to be upset and angry. Instead of focusing on the quality and the points that you're putting forward, it's about your tone and whether or not people feel attacked by what you're saying."

As a Black woman, Eyitayo described this as worrying about whether or not you're aggressive and angry, "Like that stereotype of the angry black woman. I feel like throughout my career, I constantly have that in the forefront of my mind: *will this get me blacklisted?*"

In understanding this, I realized that the process of developing a professional or academic image as a woman, let alone a woman of color, begins to resemble the process of a water treatment plant. You begin with your crude, unfiltered self: your style, your opinions, your interests. But those cannot be left as-is, God forbid you show all your cards and seem emotional, angry, or simply basic to a reader, professor, or future employer. And so, you filter: you dress for the role you want, not how you like, and you delete any online post that may compromise how employers may see you. With every article you write, or commentary you post, you edit down not just for simple grammatical mistakes, but whether your tone is too aggressive or emotional—and so it goes.

"White men really get to make careers out of having an opinion," Eyitayo reflected. "Careers of writing think-pieces and from people asking, 'Well what is your opinion on this specific policy?' And that's fine, but there's a lot of Black people that are already doing that, but instead of being uplifted for how smart and politically astute they are, people think 'Oh this person should be blacklisted, because they're really aggressive. They're too militant about their political opinions. You don't want to get into a debate with them.'"

CHAPTER 9

AT THE INTERSECTION OF FEMINISM PART 2

———

Black women have had to develop a larger vision of our society than perhaps any other group. They have had to understand white men, white women, and black men. And, they have had to understand themselves. When black women win victories, it is a boost for virtually every segment of society.

- ANGELA DAVIS

At each stage of writing and then revising this book, it felt as though the year, the seemingly-cursed 2020, could not get any worse. And yet, each time I found myself circling back to this chapter, it had.

At one of the most stressful steps in the book writing process when I was submitting my first draft of the complete manuscript, my editor connected me with another author who was publishing in December 2020 as well. Around the same age and in similar fields—Kathiana. We quickly hit it off and I began looking forward to our weekly chats.

We began working together just a few weeks before the death of George Floyd that sparked world-wide Black Lives Matter protests. In addition to the outrage and energy the movement sparked, I could see the exhaustion and heartbreak of many Black Americans whose lived experiences of racism were coming to a head with unprecedented social momentum. And, as well as in the midst of a global pandemic, both Kathiana and I were racing against our respective deadlines to get our manuscripts in on time.

I was eager to ask Kathiana how she was coping as a young, Black woman in the South, but wasn't quite sure how to bring it up. After days of outrage taking over social media, I had seen a number of posts calling out white activists for expecting their Black friends to educate them with little regard for the trauma the Black community was experiencing. Ultimately, I simply asked how she was doing and let her expand on that in however much detail she wanted.

Unsurprisingly, she was exhausted. Between writing a book and coping with increasingly intense unrest and outrage over racial disparities in the States, Kathiana told me she often felt overwhelmed. I recognized that a majority of the stories I tell in my book are those of white, or white-passing, women. The last thing I wanted was to contribute to the toxicity of what has become known as white-feminism. I needed to confront my privilege and reckon with the fact that I spoke with largely white women because I don't know enough women of color.

It's easy to repost a viral photo or article on racial injustice. It is much harder to critically look inward, recognize your own privilege, and challenge ingrained racial biases you may not even know you have. I told Kathiana how I was struggling with including WOC voices. Despite having her own manuscript to finish, she offered to tell me about her experience living as a Black woman in America.

"These past several weeks have not only been a wakeup call, but they've also been a traumatic experience because it's like my entire life I've known these things to be true and real, but it's never been realer than this moment," she explained.

Kathiana continued, reflecting on how the increase in attention toward race relations has impacted her own perspective, "And I now don't feel crazy for advocating for education for women around the world and I don't feel crazy for grinding the way that I do because there's a reason behind that." She emphasized being twenty-one with a master's degree: "That's impressive. But I'm still a Black woman in America trying to navigate the workforce."

In trying to navigate the workforce, Kathiana has struggled to maintain her own identity in a professional world that seemed to reject Black Americans more than it hired. Just to get to the interview phase, many of her family members select "other" on applications in response to race/ethnicity queries. "I don't want it to be surprising that I am successful. I want to normalize that it is ok that a Black person can achieved what it is they want to achieve in this life and to be whatever professional that they want to be," she explained.

But while Kathiana proudly highlights her race on her applications, she has been forced to suppress and conceal her identity in other ways. After receiving a message that had been sent to her, rather than the editor in chief of her publication, their security team recommended that she change her name. "My name is very unique; I could easily be found. And so I had to create an alias to go by to do correspondence which isn't the way that it should be, but there's hateful people out there, and to protect myself and those around me it was the best approach to go by another name."

Women are no strangers to writing under pseudonyms. As Virginia Woolf wrote, "For most of history, Anonymous was a woman."[15] But, as with so many aspects of the feminist movement, while we've seen advances in women's ability to publish their work without sacrificing their identity, women of color still wrestle with the concern that writing under their own name could be dangerous.

For Kathiana, this constant pressure to embrace her identity while protecting herself, her career, and her work is exhausting. "I'm at the point in my life where I want to vocalize my opinion about what's been going on," she explained in our conversation about the Black Lives Matter protests in the summer of 2020. "I feel like in the past I've been protecting an identity that's not even an identity."

I asked her what she meant. "I've been protecting my face, my name, etc. because I would refuse to allow myself to not

---

15   "For most of history, Anonymous was a woman," Austin Public Library, Accessed October 1, 2020.

get hired for supporting Black Lives Matter." Continuing she said, "I'm essentially protecting a face, a name, a person, an identity of being Black in America, an identity that's not even an identity in our society because our society doesn't look toward Black people."

Her fears exceed just being able to be hired, or receiving the odd message from a disgruntled reader, however. There is a harsh reality that all Black Americans face, a fear that has been proven time and time again.

"At the end of the day, when you step out of your workplace or your home, anything can happen, right? At any given time. And right now, the worst thing that could happen to me is to become a hashtag."

KATHIANA LEJEUNE

* * *

I knew that in writing this book, I was coming from a uniquely privileged position. As a white woman from a middle-class family, my own experiences facing down the barrel of the patriarchy are not reflective of the experiences of all American women, especially women of color. This could not have been more apparent than with the murder of Breonna Taylor—shot six times in her own bed by police officers. As I write this, her killers have yet to face justice.

For far too long, white feminism has failed to account for intersectional realities, often excluding women of color from the narrative. It took me a long time to realize, and then admit, that I was complacent in this exclusion and as I've noted in an earlier chapter, my aim for this book is to not speak on behalf of women of color, but to use this platform as a means of highlighting the problem.

Consequently, I have spent a lot of time reading and learning from Black and Latina authors, taking the time to check my own privilege. My hope is that my complacency ends with this book; that in my effort to take up space, I am making equally as much space for my Black and Latina peers and to call for change in what has largely been a movement advocating for white women only.

One of the most impactful books I've read has been *Hood Feminism: Notes From the Women That a Movement Forgot*, by Mikki Kendall. It is rightfully aggressive and directly challenges white feminists to confront their role in a movement that has largely, and at times intentionally, left women of color behind.

Kendall articulates this far better than I ever could. For example, she writes in chapter one, "a one-size-fits-all approach to feminism is damaging, because it alienates the very people it is supposed to serve, without ever managing to support them. For women of color, the expectation that we prioritise gender over race, that we treat the patriarchy as something that gives all men the same power, leaves many of us feeling isolated."[16]

---

16 Mikki Kendall, *Hood Feminism: Notes from the Women That a Movement Forgot,* (New York, NY: Viking, 2020), 12.

We cannot fail to recognise that in our efforts to progress our cause of gender equality, there are other factors that, when not properly addressed, will inhibit all women from achieving that ideal. As Kendall writes, "When feminist rhetoric is rooted in biases like racism, ableism, transmisogyny, anti-Semitism, and Islamophobia, it automatically works against marginalised women and against any concept of solidarity. It's not enough to know that other women with different experiences exist; you must also understand that they have their own feminism formed by that experience."[17]

A simple and well known example is the phenomenon of the gender wage gap. Having been used as a feminist rallying cry for years, the wage gap is one of the most obvious instances of systemic inequality. Predictably, what the mainstream feminist movement often fails to elaborate on, or at least mention, is the disparity in pay for women of color and what is called the "Emotional Tax."

It is well known that the average American woman earns eighty two cents for every dollar men make.[18] The wage gap, however, is even larger for most American women of color, with Black women earning sixty two cents for every dollar white men make and Latinas only earning fifty four cents for every dollar.[19] To paint a more detailed picture, Black women will lose, on average, $946,120 over a forty year period

---

17 Ibid, 14.
18 "Women of Color in the United States: Quick Take," *Catalyst*, accessed September 26, 2020.
19 Ibid.

because of the gender wage gap. Latinas will lose on average $1,121,440 over that same period.[20]

Kendall articulated it perfectly when she wrote, "white privilege knows no gender."[21] In addition to the literal disparity in earnings for women of color, there is the added exhaustive experience of bias and discrimination, defined by Catalyst. org as the "Emotional Tax."[22] Sixty percent of both men and women of color experience this need to be on guard against racial discrimination at their workplaces.

Again, there is no immediate and comprehensive solution to this phenomenon that could be presented tomorrow. However, as Sara Ahmed noted on representation in academia, there are simpler steps we can take as individuals to combat this. To start, we need to recognise our own privilege, whether that be gendered, racial, or regarding sexual identity, etc. To note that lines of oppression and discrimination are not mutually exclusive and then in projects confronting issues such as contemporary gender dynamics, as this book has attempted to undertake, to address related intersectionalities.

* * *

I spoke in an earlier chapter of a woman who has spent much of her life advocating for various sexual health causes and

---

20 "Women's Earnings – The Pay Gap: Quick Take," *Catalyst*, accessed September 26, 2020.

21 Mikki Kendall, *Hood Feminism: Notes from the Women That a Movement Forgot*, (New York, NY: Viking, 2020), 15.

22 "Report: Day-to-Day Experiences of Emotional Tax Among Women and Men of Color in the Workplace," *Catalyst*, accessed September 26, 2020.

abortion access. As I continued my research for this book, through interviews and various readings, the relationship between healthcare and feminism became unequivocally apparent. And it makes sense. Healthcare and political systems are inherently intertwined; and political systems and women's issues are as well.

The goal of this book is to share stories, and in turn, lessons, of contemporary gender relations largely within professional and academic spheres. And so, you may be wondering where pregnancy and birthing rights come in. Well, for one, pregnancy is seen as an obstacle to a woman's career—both by women as well as recruitment directors and others seeking new hires. But more broadly, women's bodies have been, and continue to be, policed in a way that threatens our access to simple healthcare services and perpetuates dangerous paternalistic medical practices.

As with all other avenues of feminist issues, women's healthcare is fraught with intersectional disparities, especially along racial lines. This had first come up in my discussion with Kathiana, as she spoke about her experience with systemic racism in the United States. Her mother's pregnancy and birthing process with her, after a number of previous miscarriages, was especially tumultuous. "Her water broke unbeknownst to her. She was dealing with a death in the family and her doctors just could not comprehend that. It had gotten to the point where I was suffocating inside her and she had to go into immediate delivery," Kathiana explained.

She had a sudden seizure, something that while rare can occur during a C-section, and, as she continued to bleed after the operation, she did not get the care she had needed. "But she's a survivor and can tell her story," Kathiana said. "But," she continued, "will I trust a doctor to deliver a future child? I don't think so." She paused before saying, "I wouldn't want to be in a situation where there's a doctor or nurse who doesn't understand that my pain is equivalent to someone else's."

Systemic racism within healthcare doesn't begin and end with childbirth, however. Kathiana recounted a number of times in which she's felt the direct weight of racism within healthcare herself. "I was close to having ovarian cancer," she told me after telling me the story of her birth. "I saw three different doctors before they decided to operate on me, even though the size of the cyst on my ovaries was the size of a baseball." She described that, despite severe pain she was in, her doctors continued to refuse to treat her. It was only until she went to a third specialist that ran an ultrasound and determined that she needed not just surgery, but she needed it immediately.

"That's what women mean when they say Black Lives Matter. Because they've been guinea pigs or overlooked in the medical field, despite the pain that they feel."

I was working one evening with a few of my roommates just a few weeks after moving to London. Georgie, a nursing student studying to be a midwife, read aloud a question that she had been asked on a preliminary assessment. In short, it asked what considerations one should include when caring for pregnant women from ethnic groups such as Black African and Black Caribbean communities which tend to have higher risks of hypertension and the development of type 2 diabetes than the general British population. "How am I supposed to answer that," she laughed. "It's not a biological occurrence, it's because there's so much racism in our healthcare system."

Both Georgie and another housemate of mine, Lizzie, are studying midwifery at a London university and have training shifts at local city hospitals. I had asked if they would be comfortable to do an informal interview one evening on their studies and experiences in working in women's healthcare.

Prior to our interview, Georgie loaned me Milli Hill's *Give Birth Like a Feminist*, an incredible book that outlines the importance of a woman's autonomy in her healthcare during pregnancy. Hill writes rather bluntly, "Clearly there is confusion at a global level about women's rights in childbirth and their fundamental right to bodily autonomy, the legacy of a very long history of viewing women as objects, possessions, and reproductive vessels whose destiny and fate is up to men and God and upon which they are not to be consulted."[23]

On speaking of what they've learned as midwifery students so far, Georgie and Lizzie were frank. "Pregnancy and giving birth is the most high risk medical situation you can go through as a woman in your lifetime," Georgie explained. She described birth as equally traumatic as it is beautiful and no one pregnancy and delivery experience is the same. It is messy,

---

23   Milli Hill, *Give Birth Like a Feminist: Your Body. Your Baby. Your Choices,* (London, UK: HarperCollins, 2019).

dangerous, and painful. To put any woman through that involuntarily, Georgie explained, is simply inhumane.

And the importance of consent doesn't stop once the decision is made to go through with pregnancy. Expecting mothers maintain the right to bodily autonomy before, after, and during delivery. Hill interviewed an American lawyer, who articulated this perfectly: "As Hermine Hayes-Klein put it to me [Hill]: 'How much would change in the birth room if everyone in that room really understood that the woman could not be touched without her permission...and the fact that it would be transformative tells you everything you need to know about how informed consent is routinely ignored in current maternity care systems.'"[24]

Lizzie and Georgie described over-medicalization within maternity healthcare as something that especially perpetuates that lack of understood consent. For example, episiotomies are an incision made at the bottom of the vagina to prevent tearing during labor. Up until recently, they explained, this procedure was almost routine, with women given little to no choice in this. "Even my nan and other members of my family would have routinely been cut and deformed, just for having a baby," Georgie noted. "When they are in the birthing room, many women think they are completely at the mercy of obstetricians and doctors," she said. "That shouldn't be the case."

As Hill wrote, "Birth rights are women's rights and women's rights are human rights."[25]

---

24 Ibid.
25 Ibid.

CHAPTER 10

YOU BELONG HERE

———

I'm tough, ambitious, and I know exactly what I want. If that makes me a bitch, okay.

- MADONNA

Lauren Goldberg said to me during our conversation for this book, "However much space you take up is the right amount of space." It has become one of my favorite affirmations and I have found myself repeating it more and more to myself as I continue to write. For a while, I resented that I had to remind myself of that, especially as I increasingly spoke with those who had to overcome obstacles of the socialized sexism of the '60s, '70s, and '80s to get to the positions they hold today. While today's gendered realities are much different than the norms that women like Kathy and Lauren faced at the beginning of their careers, unfair sexist standards are still very much in play.

I asked an old friend, Jackie, what she thought of being a woman in the academic and professional worlds, especially as she prepared to graduate. She told me about this incredible summer job she had managing an urban garden in New Jersey a couple of years ago. She was only nineteen, but was passionate and qualified. A large part of her job was to lead corporate work-days for local companies where they came and helped garden organic produce for surrounding communities that faced food insecurity.

"One of these work-days I stood up in front of my work group, about thirty people, and introduced myself," Jackie began.

Suddenly the director of the company stepped directly in front of her laughing and said, "Hi sweetie. I'm not sure if you know this, but we're here to help in the garden. Where is the leader for our work-day? You're too small and pretty to work here." She was taken aback.

All of his employees just stared at her in silence.

"I took a deep breath and asked him to step back with the rest of the volunteers so I could continue leading the work-day. I grabbed a shovel and repeated myself even louder." Eventually, she said, the director realized she was serious and moved back.

"Throughout the duration of the day, the female employees individually approached me to commend the way I stood up for myself," she remembered. It was clear he frequently treated women like this.

Like so many of us, Jackie confessed she often isn't taken seriously in leadership roles as a young woman. As she prepares to move on to the next stage of her career, however, she noted that it's in moments like that where her confidence in herself and her dedication to her work inspire her to overcome.

Lauren and I spoke about how she too wasn't taken seriously in the beginning of her legal career. "One of the first meetings I ever went to as an attorney, there were a bunch of older guys, I was probably thirty, and there weren't enough seats at the table." The irony in that alone was not lost on me and we laughed. "And one of the guys actually said, 'Why don't you come here…you can sit on my lap.'"

I cringed. She smiled and noted that this was before any sort of Me Too movement; twenty years ago, these things were just considered normal to say. "You know women's liberation was something that was bad," she continued. "I turned around and I said 'I don't think so. I can get my own chair,' and my boss came up to me after and said that what I had said back there was kind of rude," Lauren smirked and said, "I was like no, it's kind of rude that they would talk about me like that."

Twenty years later she is now the managing attorney of that same firm. I asked her if she could say anything to young women today just starting their careers, what would it be?

"Know yourself," she said. "In order to deal with things, you have to ask yourself where do you come from and how does that shape who you are?" Lauren especially emphasized figuring out what challenges you. Are you bad with confrontation? Do you feel like you have imposter syndrome? Do you struggle with time management?

Then take those challenges and think about how you react to them. Do you feel scared? Do you feel frustrated? And use these insights to build a realistic leadership or management plan for yourself: what you need to spend time working on, where you need to be kind to yourself, etc.

"Give as much attention to you as an individual as you do to your work and the things you're trying to accomplish," Lauren added.

She reminisced about the first case she ever handled in court. As they were walking to the courtroom, one of her mentors, who was going to be the opposing counsel, turned and looked at her; "Oh my God, you look like shit."

Embarrassed, she apologized and said she was admittedly a little nervous. They stopped and he said, "Let me tell you something. There's only two people in that courtroom that know anything about what this case is. One of them is you and one of them is me." He pointed to the bathroom and continued, "No one else has any idea so go over there, throw up, come back and go in there and show your stuff."

Lauren still remembers this moment. "Why should I have assumed I wouldn't be able to do the job?"

Which leads into her next tip: "There are two people in every interaction. You can only control one of them." You are only in charge of yourself and how you react in situations. "Don't think that other people can meet the standards you set for yourself," she concluded.

I think that is such a valuable lesson and relates to so many of the challenges women face today. You can't help that a man belittled you in a conference room full of your coworkers, but you can control your response. When faced with misogyny and contempt, we can let it slide or we can challenge and rise above it.

In recounting her experience as the first woman editor-in-chief of a major American business magazine, Rieva talked a lot about being a woman in charge in a professional environment. She explained the difficulty for women asserting leadership qualities— often, rather than being seen as a leader, they are seen as bitchy or too aggressive. "It is the women who didn't care about what others thought that ultimately succeeded in that," Rieva explained.

This advice, to not care that you're seen as bitchy or aggressive, reminds me of another part of Sara Ahmed's book, *Living a Feminist Life*. She writes, "When you speak as a feminist, you are often identified as being too reactive, as overreacting, as if all you are doing is sensationalising the facts of the matter."[26] It's a common occurrence: women taking charge or speaking out and being denoted in some way or another as too "emotional." Well, coming from some of the most successful women I've spoken to, simply put: don't care.

26 Sara Ahmed, *Living a Feminist Life*, (Durham North Carolina: Duke University Press, 2017), 21.

Lauren finished our interview with one last piece of advice for young women in the professional and academic worlds. She said the most important thing is not the prestige or the money, but that thing that you can dedicate your life to. Something that brings you joy. "Look for something that's going to fulfill you because it shouldn't be someone else doing that. Not a man, not a boss. It has to be from the inside."

Lauren's advice reminds me of a quote from Jennifer Palmieri, the 2016 Clinton Campaign Communications Director, on Hillary's concession speech: "We think a woman shines brightest when she is selflessly putting others' interests above her own." But there is so much more to a woman's success and I think that's so important to remember as young women like myself embark on the next stages of our lives. When we pursue what interests us, what we are passionate about, rather than what other's want to see us do, we will inevitably succeed. As Lauren explained, "Making the choices that feel good are the right ones, not the ones that prove something to somebody else."

That is how we take up space. That is how we go from being the subject of a sexist joke in the office to being the managing attorney. That is how we challenge the misogyny and contempt that seek to trivialize our successes as women.

Know yourself. Know what you want. And go for it.

I asked Rieva what she would say to the young women like me who are at the precipice of our careers. She thought for a moment and said, "I always thought my generation would be the one that would get there. But I think it's up to you guys." In the nineties, women's entrepreneurship exploded and she explained that in the business world, people predicted that by the year 2000, women would own half of all businesses in America. Now, in 2020, women only own about forty percent of all businesses. Of those, very few are making more than a million dollars a year compared to their male counterparts.

"But," she conceded, "I think that your generation is simultaneously more idealistic and more realistic. It's no longer just about women, it's everything. It's equality. Your generation is demanding this and you're not going to put up with businesses that don't talk the talk or walk the walk; that are not genuinely doing that right. You have the idea that there's nothing that's going to stop you."

She concluded with this: "Don't let anybody or anything intimidate you from just doing what you want to do."

As Hillary said in her concession speech, "To all the little girls who are watching this, never doubt that you are valuable and powerful and deserving of every chance and opportunity in the world to pursue and achieve your own dreams."[27]

27   Katie Reilly, "Read Hillary Clinton's Concession Speech for the 2016 Presidential Election," *Time*, November 9, 2016.

GRIT, GRACE, AND GRATITUDE

———

I am an example of what is possible when girls from the very beginning of their lives are loved and nurtured by people around them. I was surrounded by extraordinary women in my life who taught me about quiet strength and dignity.

- MICHELLE OBAMA

Writing this book has been nothing less than a labor of love. I have had the privilege to speak with countless inspiring and anything-but-ordinary women about their lives, ambitions, and role models. It wasn't until I began transcribing these conversations that I realized I had internalized so many of these stories myself. That every time I began to question the validity of this project and my abilities, I just had to read through my own notes. That there were women's' voices yearning to be heard and stories that needed to be told.

When I asked Claire about a powerful woman she looks up to, she was hesitant to say her mom. "I know you've probably heard this a thousand times and its cliche, but I would have to say my mother. If I could describe her in three words they would be: grit, grace, and gratitude." What unfolded was a remarkable story of resilience and survival. Claire's mom came from a difficult childhood, growing up under two alcoholic parents. As a university student at just nineteen, she was hospitalized with a life-threatening case of meningitis. Two doctors even told her parents to start making funeral arrangements, doubting that she would make it through the night. Nevertheless, she survived and after six long years of balancing night school and a full-time day job, she graduated with a Bachelor's degree in marketing.

Feeling as though she had to get married young to escape that household, she found herself in a new world of spousal emotional abuse. Unlike so many men and women in abusive relationships, she made the decision to leave her first husband, with two young daughters, and took on a new role as a single mother with no child support. Claire recalled times when her mom's credit card was declined trying to buy diapers at Walmart and they went to bed hungry with no means of buying new and healthy food.

When asked how she made it through, Claire's mom is frank. "For five minutes every morning I have my own pity party, then pick myself up and recognize that life goes on and I need to be here for my daughters." It was this mindset that propelled her to becoming the president of a marketing firm nearly two decades after she first began her undergraduate career. Claire recalls her drive to give her daughters the childhood she never had. Under her roof, failure, not just success, is praised. If you got an A in a class, it was probably too easy and a C showed that despite how difficult the work was, you persevered as hard as you could.

If this story sounds familiar it's because it has been told countless times in any number of ways. But a story of a single mother's grit can never be over told. I see it in my own mom every day. Whether it means driving six hours in the dead of Montreal winter to deliver soup and bagels after I had a difficult week, or waking up at 6:00 a.m. to cook a day's worth of meals for my sick brother—her ability to be constantly "on" never ceases to amaze me.

Nearly every great woman I know also comes from a family of strong, trailblazing women before her. My friend Maggie's great grandma Maryassa came to the States when she was just thirteen from a little shtetl in Romania. According to Maggie's grandma, Rosalyn, Maryassa was one of seven children whose father was killed in World War I. Jews faced frequent discrimination and were barred from going to regular school. Rosalyn's mother tried to sell food for income, but was often beaten and had her wages stolen. In Maggie's grandmother's words it was "not exactly like Fiddler on the Roof."

When she got to America, Maryassa lied about her age so she could get a job and moved in with distant family members in Philadelphia. She worked for years, got married, and saved up to bring her mother to the States too. The apartment they lived in didn't have any running water or a bathroom, but Rosalyn recalled, "When my Bubba came to this country and moved into our house, she would walk around and say she never thought she would live in a mansion."

Rosalyn is headstrong, independent, and blunt. It's no wonder considering the women she grew up around and what they faced in coming to the States. And it's clear to me that Maggie has derived much of her own independence and strength from her as well.

I too am fortunate in that I come from a lineage of incredible women. My grandma lost her own mother when she was only thirteen; and her father, my Zadie, had taken the loss extremely hard and wasn't emotionally present for the rest of her childhood. She married young, just a couple of years after high school, into a tumultuous relationship. Unable to drive and with no college education, she realized she wasn't happy. Even with two young children, she began taking classes at a local college, learned to drive, and got a full-time job in Manhattan. Then she filed for divorce.

As my mom said, so many women tend to stay within the status quo, even if they aren't necessarily happy. "With the odds stacked against them, likely no real money or credit of their own, limited work skills, family responsibilities, or just fear of their own, they just stick with the devil they know. She didn't."

It took an incredible amount of courage to change the trajectory of her life at a time when women rarely did, and in her limited circumstances; but as my grandma says, "Life's too short to be unhappy."

I grew up privileged to have such strong independent women to look up too. When I wanted to be a marine biologist, my grandma would cut out clippings from the *New York Times* science section and send them home with me. When I decided I wanted to be an astronomer, she would just save the entire section for when I came up to visit. I accumulated piles of news clippings and pages. Looking back, that support was instrumental. I was told I could be and I could do anything I wanted, and I took that to heart.

My mom equally encouraged my ambitions, even when they seemed out of reach. Family vacations were planned around the historical events I was learning about. When I became fascinated with *Liberty's Kids*, a cartoon show about the American Revolution, we went to Philadelphia to visit Betsy Ross' house and Boston to explore the Freedom Trail.

When I did a presentation on Woodrow Wilson in the fourth grade, she took me to the campus of Princeton University so I could see where he taught before he became governor and then later president. Thus, followed a brief obsession with college campuses where I insisted on touring the likes of Harvard and UPenn. My mom was always ready to go.

I can also credit my mom for my fascination with books. When I left for college, she handed me a box of books that she had been gathering since I was a baby. A collection of "must-read" titles. In the copy of *Flowers For Algernon*, she must have accidentally left a slip of paper behind that said "junior high school level (or any time!)." In the back of *The Notebook*, she wrote out page numbers where she annotated certain lines that stuck with her. Each page number had a word next to it: *love, hope, silence, life*.

In *The Tao of Pooh*, she inscribed the inner front cover. It's dated 2001. She wrote, "Read this book when everything in your life is wonderful; read it when it seems as if things couldn't get any worse. Let it carry you and let it help you unload."

I found the book and inscription just a few hours after she helped me move into my first dorm and she was well on her way back to New Jersey. When I opened it, out fell another note. In it was a list of "basics" that she had written out and been instilling in me for as long as I can remember. Among which was the following: "Everything you need to know you can find in the 100 Acre Woods." Winnie the Pooh's home.

In the final and second Winnie the Pooh book (it's our thing okay), which she had bought before I could talk, she underlined some of her favorite quotes. Among them was the same quote she used at the end of her note: "You are braver than you believe, stronger than you seem, and smarter than you think."

When I doubt myself today, I often try to think back to what my six-year-old self would do. I think of the time in Philadelphia when my family and I were on a walking tour and I answered every single question the guide posed to us by the time we got to Ben Franklin's grave, and he joked that maybe I should just lead the group. I think of when I read *Little Women* for the first time and insisted that my mom take me to Louisa May Alcott's house where I was shocked to learn that she had to publish some of her other works under a pseudonym. I thought it was absurd.

I think of the inhibition derived from growing up and realizing that some people don't want to hear women's voices. That Jo, who I related to so much, was the exception and not the rule in the beloved universe I read about. And I try to remember that these norms I've grown up with are not reality. That I still cannot, and should not, be afraid to answer all the tour guide's questions. That there are more Jo's in the world than ever and that we can do anything.

Grit—nothing comes easy. Grace—carry yourself with compassion and dignity. And gratitude—know that no matter where you are in life, even at your lowest of lows, you are always in a more fortunate position than someone else. Never forget to use your privilege to help others. And, of course, always be grateful to be a woman.

ACKNOWLEDGEMENTS

To all my family and friends who made this book possible, thank you. I especially want to thank the ultimate powerful women I've had the honor to look up to my whole life: my mom for her unwavering love, support, and extraordinary editing skills and my grandma, who is the shining example of a strong, smart, independent woman.

Thank you to my dad and brother for their encouragement and for being the laugh on the other side of the phone while I ranted about difficult peers and intense workloads. To Vivian, thank you for all of the support and the influx of surprise cupcakes and Amazon orders that provided the ultimate writing-break snacks. Thank you to the extraordinary women and sisters who have supported me from the very beginning of this process: Abby, Amy, Caitlin, Deborah, Gina, Kinza, Madeleine, and Sonia. I don't know how I've come to be so lucky as to call all of you my friends. To Lily who read the (very) rough first drafts of every chapter and who was truly my rock throughout the writing and editing process, thank you so, so much. And thank you to Erin and Mel who were among the first to share their experiences with me and whose strength is unmatched: thank you for allowing me the privilege of writing your stories.

To Eric Koester who first told me that if I put my mind to it, I really could write a book, thank you. To my editor Julie Colvin whose patience, kindness, and wisdom was instrumental in getting my manuscript to publishing, thank you. And a big thank you to the entire team at New Degree Press for everything.

Thank you to all of my interviewees, without you there would be no book. Each of your stories are a testament of your strength, resilience, and courage. In addition to those who have chosen to remain anonymous, thank you to the following individuals for your expertise and stories:

- Randi Braun
- Rieva Lesonsky
- Lauren Goldberg
- Eyitayo Kunle-Oladosu
- Kathiana LeJeune

And a massive thank you to everyone who pre-ordered *Nevertheless* and made its publishing possible:
Abby Jakus, Abi Oshins, Alice Bershtein, Amanda Croce, Amy Withington, Benjamin Cutler, Benjamin Michaels, Brian Kehoe, Brittany Stetson, Caroline Fryling, Cayce Kantor, Celia Goldfarb, Chris McNeill, Christina Su, CJ Pospisil, Claire Suisman, Dana Alison Levy, Daniella Jacobs, Danielle Quinn, Deborah Feifer, Dilse Kaygisiz, Eleanor Skladman, Elisa Branson, Elise Campbell, Elly Kaplan, Elyse Frishman, Eric Koester, Evan Goulet, Gabriella Acoury, Gina Spiridaki, Giullia Teixeira Gomes, Grace Jumbo, Hannelore Voness,

Izzy Lowenkron, Jamie Wolfe, Jasper Scott, Jessica Schiffer, Justine Stetson, Karen Williams, Kate Grantham, Katherine Dupuis, Katie Boonshoft, Katie Moskal, Kinza Hart, Kyley Jones, Leah Suchet, Lillian Blouin, Linnea Vidger, Logan Daly, Lucy Keller, Mackenzie Norton, Maddy Balliette, Madeleine Nicolas, Madeleine Wolberg, Maria Som, Marjorie Rowe, Matthew O'Connell, Maya Krieger-DeWitt, Matt Cutler, Melissa Giberson, Melissa Savoie, Michael Creager, Mikah Atkind, Molly Appleby, Nicole Stetson, Pamela Walker, Rachel Steiner, Rebecca Wu, Rena Winston, Richard Giberson, Richard Kreitner, Risa Stetson, Rita Yang, Robin Kreitner, Rosslyn Sinclair, Sammy Altman, Samuel Wendel, Sarah Thomson, Selena Yu, Simone Renaud, Sonia Bucan, Sophie Small, Sophie Tesson, Theresa Forman, Tracy Campanaro, Vivian Georgousis, and Zoe Cronin.

APPENDIX

———

INTRODUCTION

Ahmed, Sara. *Living a Feminist Life*. Durham North Carolina: Duke University Press, 2017.

Semauls, Alana. "Poor Girls are Leaving their Brothers Behind." November 2017. https://www.theatlantic.com/business/archive/2017/11/gender-education-gap/546677/

Heise, Lori, et al. "Gender inequality and restrictive gender norms: framing the challenges to health." The Lancet. May 30, 2019. https://www.thelancet.com/journals/lancet/article/PIIS0140-6736(19)30652-X/fulltext

CHAPTER 4: ...ALIENS?

Garikipati, Supriya and Uma Kambhampati. "Leading the Fight Against the Pandemic: Does Gender 'Really' Matter?" June 3, 2020. https://ssrn.com/abstract=3617953

CHAPTER 5: TRAUMA, SURVIVORSHIP AND EMPOWERMENT
Marriott BR, Lewis CC, Gobin RL. "Disclosing Traumatic Experiences: Correlates, Context, and Consequences." *Psychological Trauma: Theory, Research, Practice, and Policy* (2):141-8. March 8, 2016. https://pubmed.ncbi.nlm.nih.gov/26010111/

CHAPTER 6: LAST HIRED, FIRST FIRED
Civitella, Anabel Cossette. "Women Academics are Still Out Numbered at the Higher   Ranks." *University Affairs,* June 13, 2018. https://www.universityaffairs.ca/news/news-article/women-academics-are-still-outnumbered-at-the-higher-ranks/

CHAPTER 7: COURSE CODES AND DRESS CODES
Hillary, episode 4, "Be Our Champion, Go Away," directed by Nanette Burstein.

CHAPTER 8: AT THE INTERSECTION OF FEMINISM
Ahmed, Sara. *On Being Included.* Durham North Carolina: Duke University Press, 2012.

Ahmed, Sara. "White Men." *Feministkilljoys*, November 4, 2014. Accessed September 20, 2020. https://feministkilljoys.com/2014/11/04/white-men/

CHAPTER 9: AT THE INTERSECTION OF FEMINISM PART 2
"For most of history, Anonymous was a woman." Accessed October 1, 2020. https://library.austintexas.gov/ahc/anonymous-was-woman-58679

Hill, Milli. *Give Birth Like a Feminist: Your Body. Your Baby. Your Choices.* London, UK: HarperCollins, 2019.

"Report: Day-to-Day Experiences of Emotional Tax Among Women and Men of Color in the Workplace." *Catalyst*. February 15, 2018. Accessed September 26, 2020. https://www.catalyst.org/research/day-to-day-experiences-of-emotional-tax-among-women-and-men-of-color-in-the-workplace/

"Women's Earnings – The Pay Gap: Quick Take." *Catalyst*. March 2, 2020. Accessed September 26, 2020.

https://www.catalyst.org/research/womens-earnings-the-pay-gap/#:~:text=A%20Gender%20Wage%20Gap%20Exists,-time%2C%20year%2Dround%20workers.&text=This%20is%20compared%20to%2060.2%25%20in%201980.

"Women of Color in the United States: Quick Take." *Catalyst*. March 19, 2020. Accessed, September 26, 2020. https://www.catalyst.org/research/women-of-color-in-the-united-states/

CHAPTER 10: YOU BELONG HERE

Ahmed, Sara. *Living a Feminist Life*. Durham North Carolina: Duke University Press, 2017.

Reilly, Katie. "Read Hillary Clinton's Concession Speech for the 2016 Presidential Election." *Time*, November 9, 2016. https://time.com/4564480/read-hillary-clintons-concession-speech-full-transcript/

CPSIA information can be obtained
at www.ICGtesting.com
Printed in the USA
FSHW021934201220

9 781636 765709